The Grammar of Hindudom

The Grammar of Hindudom

Prafull Goradia

GYAN

Published, 2021

Published by

Gyan Publishing House
5, Ansari Road
Daryaganj, New Delhi-110002
Phone: 011-47034999, 9811692060
www.gyanbooks.com
E-mail: books@gyanbooks.com

Printed at: Gyan Press, Delhi.

Cataloging in Publication Data—DK
Courtesy: D.K. Agencies (P) Ltd. <docinfo@dkagencies.com>

Goradia, Prafull, author.
The grammar of Hindudom / Prafull Goradia.
pages cm
ISBN 9788121220248

1. Hinduism—Relations. 2. Hinduism and politics—India. 3. Hindutva. 4. Hindus—India. 5. Muslims—India. I. Title.

LCC BL1215.3.G67 2021 | DDC 294.5 23

Contents

1

Why this book?

The Grammar of Hindudom, is perhaps the only ideology indigenous to India, or rather to Asia. Few in the world appear to know this, leave alone appreciate it. The Indian intelligentsia often ridicules it. A few Indians and Westerners reckon that the ideology of Hindudom is the only one, if accepted by the powers that are really powerful, that can achieve enduring peace on earth. The basic purpose of this book is to explain why this would be so.

The author's intention is not to involve religion or worship here. He believes that politics is the engine of society. One does not carry one's puja into an engine whose function is to haul the train, which in this case is the society or state. If one does make this mistake, neither would a state run well nor society progress.

Here, we cannot escape being drawn to that very contentious term that lies at the root of much of the disquiet prevalent today—secularism. The credo of secularism, which has its origins in Europe, means the separation of the Church from the State. The Old Testament of the Bible had enunciated this principle. The substantial progress of

European nations began soon after they had begun implementing secularism through the Reformation in the 16th century. Countries with substantial Roman Catholic majorities, too, which awakened to this old wisdom, began undergoing progress. The French Constitution of 1905 is particularly strict about this principle.

So far, the Abrahamic religions of Judaism, Christianity and Islam have held sway in the world. These religions are based on the premise of one central figure as their God, one founding prophet and one single holy book to guide their followers, i.e., the faithful adherents of that religion.

These Abrahamic religions are based upon what can be called deductive logic. In this kind of logic or thinking, the central and defining premise is given that there is only one God, one Prophet and one Holy Book, in which all truth is contained. The followers have to mandatorily bow to and obey that God, whose message is received and explained only by His chosen Prophet and no other human being. The rules and norms of the religious and social life of the community are laid down in the Holy Book. More importantly, followers are not allowed to worship any other god, or follow any other prophet or holy book. Doing so means expulsion from the community and also often brings the punishment of death.

It would be instructive to cast a brief look at the Abrahamic family of religions. The parent is Judaism, whose adherents are Jews. Yahweh or Jehovah is the only God Jews are allowed to worship. The *Torah* is Judaism's religious scripture, whose commandments have been given by their one and only Prophet Moses. Anyone who is not a Jew is called a Gentile, to be despised and shunned. But significantly, Judaism does not welcome conversion to the faith.

The adherents of Christianity, which broke away from Judaism, are Christians. God has not been named but Jesus (Christ) is the only son of God and therefore, the only Messiah. Christianity's Holy Book is the Bible. Non-Christians are heathens or pagans, to be despised but also converted and brought into the Christian fold.

The third in the Abrahamic family is Islam, whose adherents are Muslims. Allah is the only God Muslims can worship, and Prophet Mohammad is only the prophet. The *Quran* is the holy book of the Muslims and the only book they follow. Non-Muslims are *kafirs* or infidels, to be converted to Islam by persuasion, by force or fear of death.

A possible fourth sibling in this family of religions is Marxism, founded by the 19th century German political prophet Karl Marx. Although professing to condemn religion, which Marx called the opium of the masses; Marxism itself became a religion for its followers. The political credo of communism, wherein all private property is to be abolished and means of production dispossessed by their owners and given to the people represented by the State, is the holy book *Das Kapital* written to propagate communism. Adherents of this ideology are called communists or proletarians, while non-communists are run down as bourgeois and class enemies, who have to be exterminated in a bloody class war.

Communist states like the (former) Soviet Union claimed to be secular since Marxism denied God and called religion the opiate of the masses. The presumption was that Lenin and his followers had surveyed the entire universe and found no divine presence, hence, they solemnly concluded that there was no God anywhere. In the bargain, they made Karl Marx the Red Prophet and Lenin his apostle *a'la* Peter and Paul. "Workers of the world unite" and "from each according to his ability to each according to his needs" meaning the needs of all are equal, became the holy slogans of this religion.

Marxism is transnational, if not also antinational. So is Judaism, although the number of Jews has shrunk. They were without a state until 1948. Similarly Islam abides by loyalty to the entire *ummah* or Muslim community of the world.

The opposite of deductive logic is inductive logic. There is no given premise unlike that of these religions. Ideas and postulates move from the ground upwards, evolving and developing as they travel along time. Hindu philosophy and religion are the foremost examples of this inductive approach. Hinduism does not have a founder, a single prophet or any single holy book.

The term Hindudom can loosely be used to define the Hindu way of life, both socially as well as politically, i.e., the way a polity can or ought to govern itself. A closely corresponding term is Christendom. Hindudom is not confined to modes of religious worship or social norms and customs. It encompasses the entire gamut of politics and governance.

Often apparently contrarian ideas and philosophies have grown, evolved and found their way into the Hindu fold of thought. Thus, from elaborate rituals and worship of different deities to agnosticism and atheism, all can find a place under the Hindu sun. The core guiding principles are dharma (virtue) and karma (conduct). The outcome or *bhagya* (fate) is a direct result of one's karma (good and bad).

The Abrahamic religions have engaged in conquest and domination of the world, resulting in wars, bloodshed and human suffering. In modern times, it is the cultural legacy of these religions that has spawned ideologies like capitalism, communism, Nazism, etc., which have been no different than their parents in fostering divisiveness and conflict. World War I & II, plus the Cold War, which can reasonably be called the World War III, plus global terrorism with untold human suffering, are the result of these ideologies of deductive logic.

Hindudom is the only indigenous ideology that has been born in the Asian soil, which has the capability to not only end global conflict but help human beings achieve the goal of self-actualization, which alone can bring about true inner peace. There is no other ideology rooted in the soil of Asia that has the power to do this. Even an ancient civilization like China does not have the ideological underpinning to achieve this.

China's ancient credo was based on Confucianism, which is a philosophy, a religion—a humanistic or rationalistic religion—a way of governing, or simply put, a way of life, while also laying stress on adherence to the established order of life and society, and, therefore, not to be questioned. The order comes down from heaven and preserves the world, and has to be followed by humanity. Social harmony or morality is identified as patriarchy, which is expressed in the worship of ancestors and deified progenitors in the male line. Not surprisingly, after freeing itself from European colonists and Japanese occupiers, China itself moved on to a Western ideology—communism.

Hindudom, with its inductive, integrated, hospitable and accepting philosophy is the only way of life that holds the possibility of synthesising a humanity driven by conflict into a family of nations and cultures at peace with one another. Because it is based on inductive logic, the real goal is self-actualization and inner peace; not aggression and aggrandizement.

In the old times, the king had three duties: to defend the frontiers of his kingdom, to protect his citizens from anti-social elements and to appoint a competent *yuvaraj* or successor. Religion or worship had nothing to do with governance. An example of recent times can be found in the erstwhile princely state of Travancore, whose rulers ruled as proxies of Lord Padmanabhan (Vishnu). Similar is the case with the princely state of Udaipur, whose rulers considered themselves no more than trustees of Lord Ekalinga (Shiva).

Hindudom, therefore, is malleable and flexible. The three Abrahamic religions we have discussed earlier are rigid; Judaism and Islam especially so. They are more or less uniform, simple and easy to explain, especially to a convert to Islam. Judaism does not welcome converts while Christianity does. Except this difference, all three are aggressive and expansionist. Hindudom is not even sufficiently defensive, its record is more of retreat. One says this on the basis of the fact that over 3,000 temples were desecrated and converted into mosques. Despite so many years having passed since Independence, the Hindus have not reclaimed any except the one at Ayodhya, the birthplace of Lord Rama.

It is possible that this readiness to retreat, disinclination to hit back and the fact that more or less, each temple is independent and not part of an ecclesiastical network like churches could have helped the faith avoid a fate that befell the pre-Christian European and pre-Islamic Persian and Arabian way of life. Nor has Hindudom had leaders to hold the faith together. Whoever has remained a Hindu, has remained so by inspiration and not by organisation. The inspirational nature is because it is Hindu spirituality that people find both inspiring and reassuring. It is not because of what is told to them from the pulpit by the clergy, the holy book or enforced by the fear of God. This top-down, organized approach attracts people when they feel they are in a crisis. Each of the three Abrahamic religions has thrived on the different hopes and fears of its followers. For example, Islam has not encouraged the education or empowerment of women. Christianity thrived on widespread service, whether in health or in education. Hinduism has no single grand priest to teach or guide its faithful. Numerous holy men and women provide guidance through their prayers and lectures to whoever wants it spontaneously. Nothing is done particularly to attract people; one links up with whatever one likes. In other words, Hindudom—the faith as well as the ethos—is a popular choice.

Being a Hindu is a matter of choice. There is no punishment for moving over to another sect, unlike in Islam which declares a defector to be a *murtad* or apostate. He is liable to be punished by death. In short, Hindudom has to survive and flourish on its own; not by governance, reward or punishment. It is self-rule through the spontaneous belief in one's karma by an individual. With the advent of Islamic invasion and the massive conversions of poorer Hindus to Islam, a solution was discovered by the *bhakti* saints of the Bhakti Movement—Tukaram, Ramdas, Jayadeva, Chandidas, Chaitanya, Ramananda, Namdev, Surdas, Sankaradeva, Vidyapati, Narsi Mehta, Eknath, Saraladas, Guru Nanak, Tulsidas etc. These *bhakti* saints and their teachings helped to make the faith easily comprehensible to the common folk. With them came the concept of *swami*

(Lord or Master) and *das (servant or follower).* Vedic precepts were esoteric and difficult for everyone to understand and worship. Over time, *swami* became divine or God and *das* the serf or worshipper.

Avatars like Rama and Krishna began to be treated as gods. Deities like Shiva and Brahma similarly assumed divinity as did Durga and Lakshmi. Thus, Hindudom began being taken as a polytheistic religion. In actual fact, Hinduism is neither a religion nor polytheism. At its origin and basis, it is a faith whose core is the belief in *karma* and *bhagya* (fate), deed and destiny which is as close to science and physics as can be. To drag polytheism into it was the first Abrahamic attempt to show that the faith is not far from animism, i.e., the worship of animals. By a similar allegation, the Abrahamists broke the confidence of many an Adivasi who is also a Hindu, but whose ancestors occupied the Indian space earlier than others. Many of them got converted to Christianity as a result of such propaganda. The other slogan used is that Hinduism is idolatrous — a community of idol-worshippers. Again, this was to deprive all Hindus of their self-confidence.

Yet, Hindu leaders have not countered with the question as to why every Roman Catholic church has a statue of Virgin Mary. Why does every church of every denomination have a crucifix? Islam also has been aggressive in condemning Hinduism as *butparasti* or idol-worshipping, despite the presence and reverence of the Holy Kaba in its own religion, without the circumambulation of which no Haj is complete. The Kaba was a temple with numerous idols, which the Prophet proudly destroyed when he triumphantly returned to Mecca from Medina. Why then do Muslims still pray around the temple which housed so many idols for an unknown number of years? It must have been to enable the worshipper to focus his mind while praying, and to remember it as a symbol of the divine. One can only guess that this calumny of idol worship is nothing but propaganda to divide the Hindus, i.e., a devious political strategy.

In the political sphere, Mohammad Ali Jinnah nearly snatched Assam for Pakistan in 1947 with his continual campaign that adivasis were not Hindus. As a result, the Muslims in Assam could have been counted as the single largest majority. Modern times are competitive. In 1993, American political scientist Professor Samuel Huntington had predicted a clash of civilizations. In his thesis 'The Clash of Civilizations' Huntington had stated that people's cultural and religious identities would be the primary source of conflict in post Cold War world. The early series of such a clash began in 1972 at the Munich Olympic Games in 1972 when twelve Israeli athletes were slaughtered by Islamic terrorists. In an article published in the daily newspaper *The Pioneer* in 2005, it was analysed how World War IV had commenced. This writer treats the Cold War as World War III. We have noted that Hindudom does not naturally tend towards aggression and conquest. Hence, there is all the more reason for Hindus to be aware that in this world, there could be more enemies than allies.

2

Hindu Revival Under Jihadi Provocation

The history of about 1,200 years of Islamic presence in India merits thousands of pages. For the purposes of this study, we may restrict ourselves to uncovering important but less known (or perhaps not known at all) events of this period. It is also crucial to learn about these events as they will demolish the myths spawned by Leftist-Nehruvian (and also some British) historians that Muslim invaders simply walked into India and ruled it unchallenged for over a thousand years, until the British, in turn, conquered it from them. This is contrary to the facts, presented here.

Most Indian readers fed on established—and politically correct—notions of history, would be surprised to know that it is the Hindus who resisted the onslaught of Arabs for over two centuries. This stands in contrast to the regions west and north of Arabia, which succumbed immediately to Islamization. The first Islamic attack on India happened in AD 636, but it took over 500 years for the Arabs and Turks to lay a foundation for their empire in India. Another two centuries passed before a stable empire could be formed after Akbar's reign (1556-1605 AD). The kingdom Akbar established, too, perished a century after his death.

Equally, if not more significant is the fact that the Arabs could not rule India. Actually, Arab rule in India was confined to Sind for about 150 years and a small kingdom in Mathura for a few years, although many Arab families did settle in the country. The Muslim rulers who were successful in entrenching themselves in India were mostly Turks and Afghans. Several Turk families had encroached into and settled in Afghanistan from where they came into India; their senior officials also included those from Iran.

Another fact of history to be noted is that the Turkish race originated in Central Asia, which till thirty years ago was mostly a part of the erstwhile Soviet Union. The Turks were initially imported as slaves, both domestic and military, from beyond the eastern borders of Islam in the 9th century. They gradually rose to high ranks in the military and ultimately took over the Muslim world as its empire builders. 960 AD onwards, Entire Turkish tribes were converted; these converts moved to the Middle East in waves and altered the whole demography of the region, including that of the present-day Turkey. Unlike Persia, Egypt or even the Levant, Turks accepted Islam without any reservations, sinking their national identity into it and becoming its greatest champions, relegating even the Arabs to the background. Later on, they were joined by another central Asian tribe, the mostly-Buddhist Mongols who had themselves become victims of Islam.

Dr Babasaheb Ambedkar (1891-1956) has stated in his book *Pakistan or The Partition of India*, (Vol. 8):

> These invasions of India by Muslims were as much as there were wars among the Muslims themselves. This

fact has remained hidden, because the invaders are all lumped together as Muslims without distinction. But as a matter of fact, they were Tartars, Afghans and Mongols....

They were not a loving family cemented by the feeling of Islamic brotherhood. They were deadly rivals of one another and their wars were often wars of mutual extermination. What is, however, important to bear in mind is that with all their internecine conflicts, they were all united by one common objective and that was to destroy the Hindu faith.

It should also be noted that these rulers considered the local converted Muslims as second-class Muslims. Aurangzeb, who ruled (from 1658-1707), for instance, often remarked, *'We Turks, you Hindusthanis'* to both Indian Hindus and Muslims. Even in the supposedly enlightened Mughal period (from 1526-1707), over seventy per cent of the senior administrative and military posts remained in the hands of Muslim foreigners. There are only a few instances of local Indian Muslims establishing kingdoms, for example, the Sultans of Gujarat and the Nizamshahi of Ahmednagar. There is thus no substance to the claim by Indian Muslims that they ruled over India for over a thousand years.

The resistance of the Hindus through their kingdoms, to the onslaught of Islam was both sustained and valorous. It is indeed a moot point as to how, despite Hindu valour, Muslim invaders did succeed in running over India. One must take into consideration that most accounts of the Muslim period have been written by Muslims and later by some British historians. As such, both are distorted and exaggerated in the invaders' favour.

There are several reasons for Muslim successes. The greatest fault lies in Hindus not studying the scriptures and the psychology of the invaders, which would have given them a clue to their behaviour. Hindus naively expected their ancient standards of *dharmic*, i.e., ethical warfare to be reciprocated by the invaders. Whenever Muslim invaders were defeated by Hindus, they were magnanimously pardoned *and allowed to go back.* But they used the reprieve only to regroup and attack treacherously again. Hindus never understood this. It is a lacuna that tragically still persists even to this day.

However, there is no basis to Muslim claims as well as modern-day secular myths that the British captured power from Muslim rulers or empires. *The most important conquests of the British of the cities of Delhi, Agra, Lahore and Peshawar, and the bulk of the territory they captured was from the Marathas, Sikhs and other non-Muslim rulers.* Only Bengal, Bihar and the central portion of the present-day Uttar Pradesh in India were captured from Muslim rulers.

Following the death of Prophet Muhammad, Islam's founder (570-630 AD)his successors, the Caliphs, despite internal politicking and bloodletting, expanded Islam's boundaries within the next 10-12 years to cover the territories of the two great powers of the time, the Byzantine and the Sassanid empires. Persia was conquered between 637 and 651 AD and the Islamic borders touched Afghanistan (Gandhara, i.e., today's Kandahar), which was then a part of India. Egypt fell in 641 AD. By 718 AD, Spain was conquered. Even Southern France was annexed for a few years. Within one hundred years of the Prophet's death, the Arabs became the masters of a vast region extending from the Bay of Biscay to the Indus and the frontiers of China, and from the Aral Sea to the Upper Nile.

It was, therefore, only a matter of time before Islamic expansionism turned its attention to India. Caliph Umar sent a naval expedition as early as 636 AD itself to capture the port of Thane (now a suburb of Mumbai) in India. This was the first Islamic attempt against India, but the attack was repulsed. Immediately thereafter, the ports of Bharuch in Gujarat and Debal in Sind were attacked, but the enemy was repelled. The second Arab invasion was a naval one, but the Hindu defenders not only repulsed it but also sent the Arab naval force to the bottom of the sea.

Umar wanted to avenge these defeats by attacking Makran (Baluchistan), but the Governor of Iran, Abu Musa, realising that it would be futile in view of the strength of the ruler of Sind, Chachrai, advised him that "He should no more think of Hind (India)".It should be noted that this happened at the time when the Arab armies were marching victoriously in the west. Umar wisely decided to concentrate on expanding his sway over Turkish-speaking territories of Outer Mongolia, Bukhara, Tashqand (Tashkent), Samarqand (Samarkand) etc.

Umar was succeeded by Ali as caliph. During his reign (656–661 AD), his army invaded Sind again under the leadership of General Heras. It could advance no farther than Kikan (Iran) where it was routed with severe losses incurred by the invaders. During the Caliphate of Muwahiyah, six expeditions were led by the Arabs to capture Sind, all of which were beaten back. It was only in 680 AD, after many attempts and a fierce campaign, that Makran or Baluchistan (in today's Pakistan, then a part of India) could be subjugated.

In 708 AD, a 4,000-strong Arab army under the command of Budial attacked Debal, only to suffer a rout.

A larger well- equipped force was sent under Muhammad bin Qasim, which captured Debal by treachery. Dahir, the ruler of Sind fell because of internal treachery. Muhammad captured Sind including Multan after a year in 713 AD, but he had to be recalled and there was a revival of Hindu power; the Arabs were able to retain only a toehold of land along the coastal strip. In 718 AD, Junaid, the then Governor of Sind again defeated Dahir's son and pressed forward into Gujarat and Kashmir, where he was defeated and forced to retreat by Pulakesin and Lalitaditya respectively. Thus, the Arabs were again confined only to Sind.

Subuktgin's son, the infamous Mahmud of Ghazni, grabbed power in 998 AD and ruled till his death in 1030 AD. Mahmud invaded India 17 times between AD 1001 and 1027. He first annexed territories in Persia and then turned his attention towards India. His earlier attacks were for loot and plunder and powerful Hindu rulers like the remnants of the imperial Magadhan Guptas and the Shahis of Afghanistan could contain these. Later, Mahmud's invasions were with the unmistakable aim of erasing the ancient Hindu civilization.

Mahmud's first attack was on Jaipal of Peshawar, with the Ghaznavid only narrowly managing to defeat him. However, Jaipal, unable to stomach the defeat committed suicide. When Jaipal's son Anandpal was attacked in 1008 AD, he sought the assistance of neighbouring kingdoms. The rival armies faced each other and a bitter battle ensued for over forty days. Unfortunately, just as the Hindu armies were about to win, an elephant carrying the king was frightened and fled, causing panic and disarray. But the outcome was not a victory for Mahmud as he had to hurriedly return to Ghazni because trouble brewed in his native land. He could mount his next invasion only in

1013 AD, after Anandpal's death. Mahmud was successful in eliminating his successors until 1026 AD. Thus, the Hindu Shahi kingdom that had safeguarded India's borders for 1,500 years since 500 BC now came to an end.

Mahmud's next invasions proceeded thereafter but in 1018 AD, he came up against the Chandelas, who fielded a huge army. When the Ghaznavi invader saw the size of the enemy army, he lost nerve and began to retreat. The Chandela army could have ended his saga then and there, but in one of the numerous instances of misplaced Hindu generosity, they let him escape. Mahmud later carried out his infamous desecration of the renowned Somnath Temple on the western coast of Gujarat.

The raids of Mahmud encouraged other Muslim plunderers to try their luck but the Hindus rose to the challenge. Hindu chiefs banded together and decided to repel the invaders. They joined forces, attacked the Muslim army at Kahsala and convincingly defeated it. The Ghaznavids were routed in all regions except Lahore and Multan. A major defeat they suffered was at the hands of Raja Samgramaraja of Kashmir in the 11th century, who beat back several attacks of Mahmud. Despite many attempts, Mahmud could never defeat the Kashmiri ruler. Besides, Raja Samgramaraja also helped Trilochanpala, the Hindu Shahi ruler of Kabul, with an army against Mahmud of Ghazni. Their combined army defeated Sultan Mahmud.

Salar Masood Ghazni, a nephew of Mahmud (his sister's son), attacked India in 1033 AD and reached up to Bahraich (present-day Uttar Pradesh), only to suffer a devastating defeat and death on the battlefield. Raja Bhoj, who ruled for around 50 years from 1000 to 1050 AD, played a big role in Masood's annihilation. An alliance of 17 Hindu kings led by Raja Suheldev opposed the invading Ghaznavi army and slaughtered it completely not a single soldier of Masood's army escaped, with Masood too being slain. His tomb is still there in Bahraich, venerated by ignorant Hindus by the name of 'Ghazi Baba ki Mazhar'. Raja Suheldev's statue, along with that of Raja Bhoj stands in Bahraich today.

The Hindu destruction of Salar Masood and his horde kept Islamic invaders away from the subcontinent for the next century and a half, but Hindus despite enjoying this period of peace made no effort to eliminate the marauders from the subcontinent. In fact, many Muslim merchants, *sufis* and mullahs managed to settle in various parts of the country and later acted as spies for future Muslim invaders. If today's Hindus are ignorant about how their forefathers destroyed Salar Masood in 1033 AD—a glorious episode of Indian history—it is because the Leftist-Nehruvian cabal has been successful in completely blanking it out.

Meanwhile, the Ghaznavi hold had withered away in Kabul, and they were replaced by another Turkic dynasty known as the Ghors. One of its main contenders for power, Shahbuddin Mohammad Ghori fortified Multan and invaded Gujarat in 1178 AD. Gujarat's Hindus led by the Solankis met the invading Turkic-Afghan army in the Battle of Anhilwara where they inflicted a rout on Mohammad Ghori, who escaped only by fleeing the battlefield. The Solankis of Gujarat had appealed to Emperor Prithviraj of the Chauhan dynasty that ruled Delhi and northern India during this period, to forge a joint front, but the Delhi emperor was dismissive of the idea. Eventually, Gujarat's Hindus on their own, led ably by their Queen Nayika Devi Solanki, inflicted a crushing defeat on the invading Turk army. As we have seen, Ghori escaped alive only by fleeing the battlefield.

The same Ghori later captured southern Sind and Lahore, and later grabbed the Bhatinda fort in 1189 AD because of its lax defence. Prithviraj Chauhan, enraged at this besieged Bhatinda and in the ensuing battle in 1191 AD routed Ghori, forcing him to capitulate. He then committed a ghastly blunder by pardoning Mohammad Ghori, instead of doing to him what Hindus a century and half earlier had done to the invading Salar Masood. The next year, Ghori treacherously attacked Prithviraj's army at night time, a tactic Hindus had till then not heard of. Not only did Prithviraj Chauhan pay for his blunder with his life, the Hindu empire of Delhi and northern India too was extinguished. India suffered massively for many years, with massacre of Hindus, forced conversions and slavery and also the destruction of thousands of temples. It was then that Delhi fell into the hands of the Muslims.

It can thus, be seen that the progress of Islam in the subcontinent was very slow and halting, especially when compared to its lightning sweep in West Asia and southern and eastern Europe. From 1200 AD to 1700 AD, i.e., five centuries, large parts of India did have to suffer its tyranny.

Shahbuddin Ghori's successors were slaves who were appointed to take charge of his territorial possessions. Kannauj, Jaunpur and Mirzapur had come under Ghori's control by 1197 AD, but Gujarat, which had handed him a heavy defeat, continued to resist the advance of Islam and remained independent till 1298 AD. Allauddin Khilji, who set up the Khilji Dynasty, marched upon Bihar and Bengal, which could be conquered only after tough resistance. Khilji's army, which was led by Bakhtiyar Khilji—the Islamic vandal who ransacked and burnt the ancient Nalanda University—met with defeat in Assam and was driven out from there. The Assamese king who defeated Bakhtiyar

Khilji was named Prithu. He badly wounded Khilji who became bedridden. The Ahoms stationed a strong force to counter further Muslim invasions.

Allauddin Khilji was most cruel towards Hindus, yet Hindu resistance to Islam during his rule too was unrelenting. According to Muslim chroniclers, at the peak of Khilji's rule, the life of no Muslim was considered safe outside Delhi and the city's gates would be shut at night to "prevent ambushes by the infidel". When Khilji died in 1320 AD, the law and order situation in the whole of north India was so bad that any moderate ruler from anywhere with an army of not more than 8,000-10,000 could have walked into Delhi. There were a few capable rulers in south India who could have done the job, but they used this moment to settle their personal scores rather than throw out Islamic rule. This must rank as one among the many opportunities missed by the Hindus.

The Islamic Delhi Sultanate attacked and grabbed territory all over India to save Rajputana and Assam by around 1335 AD, but could last for only about 15 years. It took another 250 years before Mughal rule could be established in Rajputana to save Mewar, which under the house of Sisodias, particularly under the legendary Hindu hero Maharana Pratap, refused to bend to Islamic rule.

Timur Lang of Samarkand invaded India in 1398 AD and carried out a brutal genocide of Hindus, but after his departure the Delhi Sultanate lay in a state of anarchy. Islamic commanders plundered the countryside, but Hindus too retaliated. The city of Jalandhar in Punjab was retaken by Hindus in 1431 AD and all Muslims there made prisoner. A Muslim historian Yahya bin Ahmad wrote that the "ruthless infidels had absolutely no respect for the religion of the Mussalman". But Hindus failed to find effective leaders in this phase when the Sultanate in Delhi was tottering.

Maharana Kumbhakarna Singh (1433-1468 AD), more popularly known as Rana Kumbha, emerged as a mighty and invincible Hindu monarch. A staunch Hindu, Kumbha defeated the sultans of Gujarat, Malwa and Gwalior individually and jointly. Such was the awe he aroused that not even the Delhi Sultanate dared send an expedition against him. Kumbha not only remained unvanquished throughout his life, but also defeated every Islamic invasion against him. Had all Rajput clans united under his banner, he would have erased Muslim rule from India. Sadly, this did not materialize. It was Kumbha who built the famous Victory Tower at Chittorgarh near Udaipur.

Maharana Sangram Singh, or Rana Sanga (1482-1528 AD) as he was known, was another powerful Rajput king. He ruled a powerful Rajput confederacy. Sanga's might can be gauged by the fact that he gave Delhi's Sultan Ibrahim Lodhi a comprehensive thrashing twice, and also defeated the joint armies of the Gujarat and Malwa sultanates. Yet, despite showing Ibrahim Lodhi who was the boss, Sanga had no qualms about letting the Uzbeg adventurer Babar invade Delhi. The Lodhi Dynasty was extinguished in the First Battle of Panipat in 1526. Babar then clashed with Sanga, but his Mughals were badly routed in the first encounter. Only a Rajput traitor Silhadi's defection to the Mughal camp enabled Babar to defeat Sanga in the second encounter. Many historians estimate that even after this defection, had Babar not possessed canons, Rana Sanga would have ended his story that day. Yet, Sanga made no effort to build any ties with Delhi's Rajputs, many of whom served under Ibrahim Lodhi. Ironically, one of Ibrahim's nephews Mahmud Lodhi, who hated Babar and sought his destruction, allied with

Sanga in his war against Babar and perished. This was yet another Hindu opportunity gone abegging.

In 1336 AD, two Hindu brothers, Harihara and Bukka, founded what went on to become the great Vijaynagara Empire in the south of India. This liberated a large part of southern India from Muslim tyranny. During the time of Krishnadevaraya (1509-1529 AD), the Vijayanagara Empire stretched from Cuttack in the east to Goa in the west, from Raichur in the north to the Indian Ocean in the south. But Hindus did not make use of this great opportunity to erase Islamic rule. Later, weak successors of Krishnadevaraya and the suicidal policy of recruiting Muslim soldiers in the army led to invasion by the combined armies of the Bahmani sultans, and the empire's downfall after the Battle of Talikota in 1565 AD. Muslim soldiers defected enmasse in this battle. This is all the more galling when one looks at the map of India in 1526 AD. A far lesser part of India was ruled by Muslim rulers, as compared to 1335 AD. Hindus had reconquered a large part of India.

The Bijapur Sultanate's most able commander was Shahji Bhonsale. Upon his shoulders rested the power of the sultanate. He failed to see the opportunity to build his own power base. His son Shivaji was quick to see the opportunity and he grabbed it, and thus, created history, not only rescuing Hindu dharma but eventually going on to build a kingdom that one day erased Mughal domination in India. Shivaji proved to be a rare Hindu ruler.

Mughal emperor Aurangzeb (1617-1707) was the ultimate in Islamic zealotry, intolerance and jihad upon the Hindus. But the military might of his empire rested on the valour and foresight of his Rajput vassal Mirza Raja Jai Singh of Amer. Jai Singh commanded a pan-Rajput stature and respect. Had he rebelled against Aurangzeb, the story of the Mughals would have been over much earlier. But such was Jai Singh's misplaced sense of loyalty that he even declared Aurangzeb to be an avatar of Lord Vishnu!

Eventually, when the Rajputs did rise against the Mughals from 1650-1660 AD onwards, they first refused to join the Mughals in their war against the Marathas and later aligned with the latter. The result was that the Mughals were not only defeated in the Deccan and central India, but their rule over Rajputana too collapsed, with Awadh also passing first into Maratha and later British suzerainty. Besides, Aurangzeb's invading army was put to rout in the Battle of Saraighat in 1668 AD by the legendary Ahom general and hero Lachit Barphukan. The Mughals remained confined to Delhi and Palam, until Bahadur Shah Zafar was dethroned following the failure of the Mutiny in 1857 and packed off to die in exile in Burma. This was the formal end of Muslim rule in India. But had Hindus made use of the many opportunities that came their way, Islamic rule might have ended much earlier.

Given this history and tradition of Hindu resistance to Islamic rule, readers and students will no doubt query as to why so little by way of history was written by Hindus. In other words, why do we not have access to extensive Hindu records and why we had to wait until the advent of the British and subsequently their officers, scholars and historians? Muslim invaders had their chroniclers who extolled the exploits of their masters. The medieval period is a catalogue of one Muslim invasion after another and in popular perception, each time the Hindu/Indian defenders were on the losing side. The tactical or the battlefield causes of each defeat are given. But the question of why Hindus, despite never giving up their resistance to Islamic domination, had to endure it for another five hundred years has seldom been asked.

It cannot also be denied that the sagas of valour and sacrifice by Hindus in safeguarding their civilization have been deliberately ignored by 'secular' and Marxist historians, whose stranglehold on the academia, media and other citadels of power was facilitated by India's first Prime Minister Jawaharlal Nehru, whose own rise to power was most undemocratic. He was thrust upon the post-British India by none other than Mahatma Gandhi despite Sardar Vallabhbhai Patel being the unanimous choice in the 1946 Congress party's presidential elections, a decision which had far-reaching consequences for Hindus, particularly so in the realm of perception and narrative.

This is not to say that Hindus did no work in recording the saga of their civilization. There have been numerous records; some still survive, but most have been lost to the vicissitudes of times and the rule of invaders who ravaged this land. Let us just cast a look at one incident of how the literature of ancient Indian history was systematically destroyed. Bakhtiyar Khilji, a prime henchman of the Delhi Khilji sultanate, burnt the library at Nalanda University in 1193. With this, all the ancient texts including historical records that were collected there since 500 AD were lost. These texts covered a whole world of knowledge from agriculture to metallurgy, medicine to astronomy and of course, politics and spiritualism.

In addition, in the case of the Marathas, all original documents dealing with the life and times of the great Shivaji were lost when the Mughals under Aurangzeb, in the initial years of their long but failed Deccan campaign (1680-1707), burnt those documents. In November 1689, when the

Mughals managed to enter Raigad, they burnt the entire records of the Maratha kingdom. Today, when one wants to piece together the history one has to painstakingly use multiple private sources where letters and documents of that period can still be found.

While Islamic vandalism is easily identifiable as the culprit in the targeting of ancient Hindu records, it is equally important to learn that the British have not been free of this crime, either. The British overcame the Marathas in the Third Anglo-Maratha war in 1818, and soon went about systematically denying the Marathas' historical legacy. This is just one example.

Sir Jadunath Sarkar is regarded as an authority on Maratha history, who to his credit has done outstanding work. The fact however, remains that Sarkar did not know Marathi. What he and most of other writers had to rely on was their knowledge of English and Indian history as recorded by the British. It goes without saying that most of the history written by these worthies was regurgitated writings of Western scholars who had taken the trouble to master the local languages. Most Indian scholars and academicians of that colonial era simply did not. What we have therefore, is the colonial rulers' version of Hindu history, which has been tailored to portray Hindus as a perennially beaten race, which as we can see, is falsehood.

Hindu cultural and civilizational expansion in South-East Asia, mainly by Chola and Pallava kings from the present Tamil Nadu, is only vaguely known. There is a six feet tall and three feet wide stone tablet in the Pallava script in the national museum in Jakarta (Indonesia). We have not found the time or resources to translate the contents into Bhasa Indonesia and/or English.

This has given a handle to the 'modern' historians in India to question every single historical fact. 'Modern' researchers have also made it a dogma of their faith—which is nothing but an offshoot of Western religions deriving from deductive logic, which admits to only its own given premises. This is to dismiss the memories of the past preserved in an oral tradition or as a part of the word of mouth knowledge passed on from generation to generation, which is an inalienable part of Hindu tradition and indeed, all ancient Eastern civilizations.

Luckily for Hindus, the Buddhist monks who spread all over Asia—Sri Lanka, Indonesia, China and Japan—carried much of the ancient texts with them. These now await Hindu scholars. After 70 years of suffering successive regimes that were hostile to any Hindu revival, we today have a government that is committed to cultural nationalism. It is for it to take steps to tap these sources and restore the lost knowledge of the Hindus.

3

Hinduism and Other Faiths

In the early 1990s, I used to visit Mumbai often on business tour and would take a taxi from Santa Cruz airport to the hotel in the south of the city. Often the taxi drivers hailed from somewhere in UP and spoke Hindi or simple Urdu. The most frequently discussed subject in those years was the Babri edifice at Ayodhya. The Urdu speaking drivers tended to mistake my religion and often opened the doors of their hearts. If Ayodhya was uppermost on their mind, they wanted *inteqam* or revenge; until then they could not sleep in peace. If I asked whether it was worth shedding blood for the sake of fallen stones, the answer was quick; blood and flesh are given to man in order to defend his faith. If he cannot do this duty, what was his blood worth? A typical comment of a Hindi-speaking taxi driver was that what happened on 6 December 1992 was the work of *punya* (sacred deed), especially because no life was lost on that day. No Hindu sacrifice was too great for the sake of retrieving Bhagwan Rama's birthplace. He did not quite see the contradiction between no life being lost and no sacrifice being too great. Nevertheless, the aversion to destroying life explained the long time it took to retrieve the birthplace, no matter whose government it was, whether at Lucknow or in Delhi. Questioning one of the taxi drivers once did bring out that in order to do a *punya* one should not commit a *paap* or a sin. To a Muslim, Christian or a Jew, these conversations might give the impression that the Hindu was a coward or at least a confused person or perhaps a fatalist. The birthplace would be recovered when it was fated to; it was not right to commit violence to retrieve even the Ram janmabhoomi. On the other hand, the Urdu-speaker came through to everyone as very clear and decisive.

Those who happened to have pondered with sympathy and seriousness have realised that the root of no faith is closer to science than that of Hinduism. The root of the Sanatana Dharma (eternal faith) is karma or action whose effect is *bhagya*. In English, it would be 'one's deeds leads to one's destiny'. In terms of science, especially physics, this would mean "every action has an equal and opposite reaction". How much closer can the relation of human and divine be to science? Yet, Hinduism often has been dismissed as fatalistic, a calumny that has not been contested by Hindu scholars. Karma is the seed or core of Hinduism. The rest of Hinduism is the outgrowth that has flowered and flourished over thousands of years. Politics, in theory and practice, have been the most recent buds and shoots of that growth. To go back to the first seed, it was sown spontaneously and not by any prophet like Muhammad or a godhead like Jesus Christ. Islam, Christianity as well as Judaism (whose god is Jehovah) grew and spread deliberately and in a guided manner.

Hinduism, on the other hand, remained an impromptu phenomenon, so free that at times it has been as if the same tree but has different branches that produce flowers of different colours. The faith has broadly two devotional systems — Shaivism or Shiva worship and Vaishnavism or Vishnu worship. Each of these two systems has subdivisions, like the latter has devotees who call themselves Swaminarayan. These devotees are the ones who have built the series of Akshardham grand temples in different countries. ISKCON is another; it is an American sponsored organization doing wonderful work, in many countries. Most temples are independent and not parts of any series or organisations. Jainism is possibly nearer the original Vedic beliefs and in some ways represents the essence of Hindu philosophy. The Jains believe there were 24 *Tirthankaras* or enlightened, immortal souls, the last of whom was Mahavira, the first being Rishabhadeva. One sect is called *Digambar* which means the sky is the dress; their holy men do not wear any clothes. To go about perpetually without being dressed requires endurance, courage and, above all, a surrender of the ego. Then there is a sect which calls itself *Shwetambar*, i.e., white robed. They also believe in penance as devotion.

On the other hand, Buddhism proved much simpler to understand and to practice. Incidentally, both the faiths began in what is today's state of Bihar and also at about the same time; say, some twenty-six centuries ago. Siddhartha Gautama travelled and preached for some fifty years. He became so popular to the extent that much before he ascended to *nirvana* or salvation, he was looked upon as God. Hindus look upon him as the ninth avatar of Vishnu although Gautama, referred to as Buddha after his Enlightenment, never brought up the subject of the divine. Herein, there lies a commonality between the intellectual Jainism and popular Buddhism, as with pristine Hinduism, which stresses karma and not God.

The core of Buddhism stresses suffering, which is caused by attachment, which in turn is a result of the inevitable karma. There is no escape from karma so long as there is birth, death and rebirth. The Buddha, therefore, stressed the urgency of attaining Nirvana or salvation. He recommended the pursuit of an Eightfold Path ranging from right thought to right living. The truths behind the Eightfold Path are often referred to as *dhamma* in Pali and (dharma in Sanskrit). The Hindus call this law of cause and effect karma and *bhagya*. Evidently, the thinking was clear and scientific. Theological differences resulted in sub-denominations such as the Hinayana, Mahayana and Vajrayana sects.

It is evident from the above narration that Hinduism, Jainism and Buddhism are sisters born of the same parent. What is remarkable is that there have been, and continue to be arguments among leaders of those faiths, but no physical clashes. This is in sharp contrast to how the three Abrahamic offspring, namely Judaism, Christianity and Islam dealt with one another. Jesus Christ was born a Jew and died a Jew, and yet Christians to this day, have not ceased to be anti-Jewish. The eight crusades in the Christian endeavour to retrieve their holy land are legendary.

The two parallel histories — of the Eastern faiths and their preference for non-violence, and the interactions of the three Abrahamic religions and their propensity for violence show a remarkable contrast. To try and read one trilogy through the eyes of the other would be misleading. There have been towering scholars who have understood this syndrome. Sir Arnold Toynbee, the renowned British historian has been one such philosopher of history.

The tolerance of Hinduism was recognised by Toynbee, who on many occasions contrasted the exclusivity of the

Jewish religion, based on the Jewish belief that the Jews are the chosen people, with the large tolerance of the Hindus and Buddhists. This plague of exclusiveness, he claimed, was inherited by both the Christians and Muslims: hence, their lamentable record.To quote Toynbee:

> It is already becoming clear that a chapter which had a Western beginning will have to have an Indian ending if it is not to end in self-destruction of the human race. At this supremely dangerous moment in human history, the only way of salvation is the ancient Hindu way. Here we have the attitude and spirit that can make it possible for the human race to grow together into a single family. So now we turn to India. This spiritual gift, that makes a man human, is still alive in Indian souls. Go on giving the world Indian examples of it. Nothing else can do so much to help mankind to save itself from destruction.
>
> There may or may not be only one single absolute truth and only one single ultimate way of salvation. We do not know. But we do know that there are more approaches to truth than one, and more means of salvation than one. This is a hard saying for adherents of the higher religions of the Judaic family (Judaism, Christianity, and Islam), but it is a truism for Hindus. The spirit of mutual goodwill esteem, and veritable love is the traditional spirit of the religions of the Indian family. This is one of India's gifts to the world.

Toynbee acknowledged the gift of India but did not detail the reason why Hinduism and its political corollary could help the world achieve universal peace. The Judaic or Abrahamic family of religions induced collective unity, which in turn would blossom into national ambition to conquer or dominate other nations. In other words, the religions of Abraham were prone to inspire imperialism, which in turn would lead to war or violence.

This is not to pick on these three religions, but to illustrate the motive force behind collective unity. Much before them, Zoroastrianism flourished in Persia. Its Book is the *Zend Avesta*; its prophet was Zarathushtra and above all, its godhead is Ahura Mazda; one Book, one Prophet, one God, equally characteristic of the Abrahamic religions. Uncannily, the Persian Empire under a number of its emperors repeatedly went to war, especially against the Hellenic world. The motivation behind the three "Ones" is to bring more people and power under the umbrella of their god. That is the price one has to be prepared to pay for an ideology based on deductive logic. Under this system of reasoning, one begins with a given or invented premise such as Ahura Mazda, Yahweh, Jesus and Allah being the only gods to be worshipped for the Zoroastrians, Jews, Christians and Muslims respectively. Any follower of these religious cults begins his/her life with the acceptance of this god, logically followed by the teachings of the nominated prophet. The increase in the number of followers is the next stage in the deductive scheme of the religion.

The further logical corollaries flow steadily and smoothly, like the river Nile does through Egypt. There may be a debate or deviation over a corollary or two, but never on the three "Ones". Conquest or domination is the opposite of peace. Domination, however long-lasting, is possible under such deductive dispensations, but not peace, which demands a commitment or a belief in non-violence. Without this commitment on a civilizational scale, expansion and war would keep crossing the minds of the rulers and their class. A true Hindu would fight in defence of himself, his people and his country, but would not wish to commit aggression in order to either capture or dominate. His utopia lies in self-actualization or a life studded with one karma more shining than the previous one. The true Hindu does not believe that he can attain *mukti* or salvation without laudable karma. Victories on the battlefield, or the multiplication of his territory have no value unless achieved in the defence of his motherland.

4

Hindudom and Other Ideologies

Karl Marx, one of the world's foremost ideologues propagated that communism means a system wherein a human being would contribute "each according to his ability" and obtain "each according to his needs". In saying so, he presumed that human needs are almost equal. Marx evidently focused only on physical needs. But what about intellectual, emotional, and above all, motivational needs? There is no denying that human beings differ a great deal from one another. Marx's fixation was so much on the material that he overlooked most other facets of life. After all, he became famous for his thesis on the materialistic interpretation of history, which along with his masterly critique on capitalism forms the substance of his magnum opus *Das Kapital* (The Capital).

However, the ideology and practice of communism had a short life, less than a century, largely because of Marx's inadequate understanding of human nature. He forgot the old adage that man does not live by bread alone. In sharp contrast, Prophet Mohammad was a genius when it came to psychology. In a man's world, he gave him all the basic things he could have wanted; for example, as many women as he wanted, as many slaves as he could capture and maintain, as much land as he could conquer and keep as *wakf* forever, study as much as he liked or as little as he cared to. As a result, Islam was expanding in numbers even fourteen centuries after its birth. Now that the man's world is ending and women are rising, Islamic bigwigs would have to discover new responses to the challenges of modernity.

To Karl Marx, capitalism would have been "from each according to his ability to each according to his wealth". The Bible clarifies by stating "render unto God what is His and unto Caesar what is his". It logically followed that the leaders of Christianity meant to let the trader pursue his vocation as he wished. This original distribution of functions gave the religion of Jesus Christ the versatility a civilization requires to keep growing and flourishing. Unlike Islam which retained a stranglehold on its followers (for example, apostasy is punishable by death), Christianity allowed more freedom to its believers and, therefore, could scatter into many denominations. Nevertheless, Christians have respected their faith, particularly one of its important dogmas; namely that God made Man equal but the vagaries of society make him unequal. To make up, Christians promote more charities, hospitals, schools and universities than any other community.

Socialism, a favourite ideology of many a political party, was defined by Marx as "from each according to his ability, to each according to his opportunity". There is justice personified in this ideology. Ability is God-given but society must give every member an equal chance to blossom; not keep anyone down or at a disadvantage. The question is how consistently has socialism been practised and in how many places.

Any ideology that emanates from Hinduism must have at its core the actions and their reactions of every *jeevatma* or living being, whether in the current birth or a previous one. Marx, had he defined this, would probably have said "from each according to his karma, to each according to his *bhagya*". The destiny of each being would be determined by the deeds of that being, whether in this life or a previous one. Conceptually, it is similar to a foundational principle of physics—for every action, there is an equal and opposite reaction. It embodies unquestionable justice as well as science at its precise best. Perhaps, the only imponderable is the Hindu theory of the transmigration of souls from one birth to another. It is ultimately a challenge of faith. My own experience has been that approximately three-quarters of my life has been an equation of karma and *bhagya*. The remaining quarter is a matter of faith in the karmas of my previous lives or births. I reckon that if three-fourths is true, why not the remaining quarter? Even the most dedicated scientist lives on some faith at least. For example, maternity is usually a known fact but how many can vouch for one's paternity?

The question of faith leads us to the fact that Abrahamic religions are far more demanding than Hinduism. The latter relies on karma or one's own deeds and the resulting reward or punishment, whereas the former insist on the follower accepting Jehovah, Jesus or Allah as the only god of that religion. The slight difference in Christianity is that Jesus Christ is looked upon as the son of God rather than God himself. There is no variation permissible in adherence to these godheads. The theology of Judaism is not known to have varied since its beginning. Islam disapproves of variations; *ijtehad* or reinterpretation was prohibited about a thousand years ago, after which *taqlid* or orthodoxy has been the way of Islam. Christianity has permitted differences from as early as the 4th century AD, when the Orthodox Church was founded in Constantinople, as distinct from the Vatican. The Reformation began in the 16th century; since then the Church has split into dozens of denominations.

Essentially, these three Abrahamic religions would be categorised by the discipline of logic as deductive. The basic premise is enunciated in the *Torah,* the *Bible* and the *Quran.* The rest of what is right or wrong flows from the premise like the corollaries of deductive logic. They are consistent and make life easy to lead for the follower, if he is faithful. The discipline is like "Yours is to do or die but not to question why". The premise is given, the corollaries are logical and an undue violation would be treated as apostasy.

The Abrahamic religions, we have seen, are deductive in their logic. They begin with a premise and work downwards. On the other hand, the Hindu view is inductive in its logic, which moves from facts on the ground upwards till it reaches a conclusion. To illustrate this difference, let us suppose that four Hindus happen to meet and each one of them is from a different region of the country. The person from Punjab happens to declare roses to be red. The man from Tamil Nadu says he has seen only white roses; the one from Bengal disagrees, for he has seen only yellow roses and the Maharashtrian knows of only pink roses. They might argue for a while, then unable to conclude unanimously, they agree to disagree saying, "maybe roses are so in your part of the country". They do not fight or quarrel. On the other hand, an Abrahamic may declare the rose alien to him as a weed or perhaps a flower other than a rose. That is a deductive attitude based on the premise that the colour of a rose can only be red. The inductive approach of the Hindu would accept that the ground reality elsewhere could be different and hence, agree to disagree. One of the four could say that he has seen only yellow roses, but maybe in the other areas of the country there are other colours.

Hinduism does not have a book as its fountain of belief; there is no premise and, therefore, no corollaries which a follower can refer to, or a commandment or guidance. Nor do Hindus have an ecclesiology or a network of clergy or bureaucracy, either for worship or administration. There are a few groups of temples, but mostly each temple is an independent entity with its own priests connected with no other. As is well known, there are numerous deities and avatars which Hindus worship. In other words, other than karma, Hinduism has no uniformity nor a unity of worship. In fact, Hinduism is a paradise of diversity. That is why it is not a religion but a way of life anchored on karma and, of course, a few broad groups like the Shaivites, Vaishnavas, Shaktas, et al. For much of their lives, worshippers are not even aware which group they belong to. One outstanding feature of the faith is its reverence for female deities, whether Durga, Kali, Lakshmi, Saraswati and many others.

5

Hindudom and Hindu Nationalism

What is the necessity for Hindu nationalism, is a query many liberals and moderates, not necessarily anti-Hindu, are likely to raise. A nationalism underpinned by the grammar of Hindudom is imperative as Hinduism is the only living ancient religion in the modern world. India's neighbour China is perhaps the only country that can claim an ancient civilization. Today's Chinese, however, are not very aware of the heritage of their ancestors, and China's rulers even less so. Hinduism thus, is the only socio-cultural construct that has the wherewithal to challenge the domination of the ideologies and systems spawned by religions originating from deductive logic.

Domestic political movements in India between the two world wars were mainly about the freedom movement against British colonial rule. But there were also substantially concerned with variations of Hindu nationalism, which was slowly but surely rising to unify and strengthen Indian society against the threat of other cultures (Islam and Christianity), while seeking to fill Hindu society with confidence and instill in them a sense of a higher mission than merely evicting the British rulers from the country. These movements of Hindudom originated in Maharashtra but grew to be strongest in northern India, where the Muslim threat was more acutely perceived and Islamic separatism was growing in stridency.

The political activism in the country following the end of the First World War, one of whose consequences was the end of the 800-years-old Ottoman (Islamic) Empire, lent increasing grist to the politics of Islamic separatism. The fall of the Ottoman Empire was not just the end of an Islamic sultanate, but also of the Islamic Caliphate. The Sultan of Turkey had for centuries been also the Caliph and, therefore, the leader of the Muslim (Sunni) *ummah* (worldwide community of Muslims). Following Turkey's defeat along with that of the Axis powers in WWI, there was internal upheaval in that country, at the end of which its reformist leader Kemal Ataturk rose to ascendancy and abolished the Caliphate forever in 1924, also exiling the deposed Sultan Abdul Hamid II.

The end of the centuries-old Islamic Caliphate was a death knell for Muslims worldwide and set off a virulent churn among Muslims in India as well. The Khilafat Movement, also known as the Indian Muslim movement (1919–1924), was a pan-Islamist political protest campaign launched by Muslims of India to restore the deposed Caliph of the Ottoman Caliphate, who was considered the leader of Sunni Muslims. The leaders of the Khilafat Movement were Shaukat Ali, Maulana Mohammad Ali Jauhar, Hakim Ajmal Khan, and even Maulana Abul Kalam Azad.

Although political activities and popular outcry on behalf of the Caliphate emerged across the Muslim world, the most strident advocacy and activism for its restoration was in India. This also left a trail of blood. Muslim fanatics were inflamed by what they regarded as a body blow to pan-Islam. The collapse of the Congress-Khilafat (Muslim) alliance after Gandhi's unilateral withdrawal of the Non-Co-operation Movement in 1922 was followed by intense rioting and polarizing of Hindus and Muslims into conflicting camps.

The Khilafat Movement itself collapsed by late 1922.The worst riots were the Moplah riots in Kerala's Malabar region, in which hundreds of Hindus were murdered, their temples desecrated and women outraged. The silence of the Congress and the refusal of Gandhi to even condemn the Muslim perpetrators (Gandhi went to the extent of whitewashing the Moplah rioters by saying "they were only following their religion" and sermonizing Hindus to "face death bravely" but never retaliate) became a driving reason for increasing Hindu consolidation, also brought on by growing Hindu realisation that Gandhi's Congress could not be trusted to protect Hindu interests.

Hindu counter-polarization had already begun as early as 1905 with the first partition of Bengal (Bang-Bhang), with localised forerunners emerging in both Bengal and Punjab during the period 1905-1909. These grew into Hindu nationalist movements in the form of the Hindu Mahasabha, founded in 1915 and the Rashtriya Swayamsevak Sangh (RSS) founded on Vijayadashami day in 1925,and began growing rapidly in direct response to growing Muslim obduracy.

Both these movements had begun in the early 1920s against a background of massive communalisation of Indian political life. The Arya Samaj, a Hindu reforming sect of the mid-19th century, championed the Aryans of the Vedic era, and the Hindu Sabha had already begun to channel these ideas into proto-Hindu nationalism in the Punjab by 1910. However, it was the launch in 1923 of the Hindutva idea by the veteran patriot V D Savarkar (who later also became the president of the Hindu Mahasabha), that this ideology crystallised into an ethnic nationalism. Savarkar's career of anti-British revolutionary extremism and his writings on Indian history, Hindu identity and destiny inspired Dr Keshav Baliram Hedgewar from Nagpur to form the RSS, an organisation intended to reinvigorate the nation through an awareness of India's glorious past, Hindu piety, paramilitary training and sports.

At this time Hinduism in India was also directly affected by the political institutions of British rule. The principle of communal representation became general in the Award of 1932, which made provision for Muslim representation in state legislatures by quotas based on the numbers of each religious group in the population. The new Hindu political organisations sought to address this problem of declining Hindu influence by seeking conversions among non-Hindus and the return to the fold of former apostates through Hindu Missions.

Vinayak Damodar Savarkar (1883–1966) was born into a middle class Chitpavan Brahmin family in the village of Bhagur near Nasik in the province of Maharashtra in western India. He was an early adherent to the cause of Indian independence. Savarkar admired the Chaphekar brothers who had assassinated a British administrator at Poona in 1897 and gone to their execution singing verses from the *Bhagavad Gita*; deeply impressed, he took an oath before his family deity to fight for India's freedom. By 1899, he had begun his career of anti-British conspiracy with the founding of secret societies. He went on to make patriotic speeches and organize demonstrations over the 1905 partition of Bengal. A high academic achiever, he won a scholarship in 1906 that enabled him to study in London, where he became a leading figure at the India House. Here he continued his revolutionary activities, raising political consciousness among other expatriate Indian students and learning how to make bombs. Savarkar published his first book, *The War of Indian Independence* (1909), to commemorate the fiftieth anniversary of the Indian Mutiny but it was promptly suppressed by the British government.

Meanwhile, a member of Savarkar's group (Madanlal Dhingra) was convicted of assassinating Sir Curzon Wyllie in London, after his own brother Ganesh was sentenced to transportation in 1909 for armed activities. In 1910, Jackson, the collector of Nasik was gunned down in revenge for the brother's sentence, and Savarkar was arrested in London for complicity in the murder. Extradited to India, he was convicted of treason and of being an accessory to murder and sentenced to two consecutive life-transportations. He served ten years in jail on the Andaman Islands, from 1911 to 1921, and three further years in prisons at Yervada, Nasik, and Ratnagiri. Savarkar used the period of his confinement for writing and became a prolific author, publishing thirty-eight books in the course of his lifetime. These included poetry, essays, and an autobiography in Marathi. The treatise on the 1857 Indian Mutiny and an account of his transportation and prison sketches in the Andamans were published in English.

In the Ratnagiri prison, Savarkar wrote his famous short work *Hindutva* (1923), which set out his view of Indian history from a Hindu point of view and his conception of Hinduness. A preface posed the question "Who is a Hindu?" and stated, "A Hindu means a person, who regards this Land of Bharatvarsha, from the Indus to the Seas as his Fatherland as well as his HolyLand". The work was inspired by his own spirit, bold generalization and is replete with heroic quotations, which struck a chord with those who believed in Hindutva.

Savarkar's broad canvas of Indian history found a particular focus in the zenith and decline of the Mughal Empire between 1560 and 1760. The rise of Maratha power, first in Maharashtra and later throughout India, challenged and finally destroyed the Mughal Empire, ending the long period of Muslim rule in India. Savarkar regarded this Maratha ascendancy as the most important movement of Hindu liberation in Indian history. The Maratha challenge to the impressive and long-standing edifice of Mughal authority also struck him as an inspiring precedent and prelude to his own campaign to drive out the British, the founders of another secure and magnificent Indian empire. At the same time, the increasing tensions with the Muslims were an obvious factor in his ideology.

The rise of the Marathas is undoubtedly one of the significant epochs of Indian history. This small race of sturdy individuals renowned for their hardiness, perseverance and industry was drawn mostly from what might be called the cultivator class, and their leader (*peshwa*) was usually from the small minority of the Brahmin class. The Marathas first entered history through their intrepid leader Shivaji (1627–1680), who began his career by grabbing territories under the control of the southern Bijapur Adilshahi Sultanate. Soon, Shivaji controlled a sizeable territory. He struck a body blow to the sultanate by slaying its powerful commander Afzal Khan in 1659, also destroying his forces. The rich Mughal port of Surat was sacked by Shivaji's Marathas in 1664. Realising that the son of Shahji Bhonsale was no local threat, Aurangzeb appointed his son, Prince Muazzam, to command his army in the Deccan against the Marathas. Associated with the prince in this campaign was Raja Jai Singh of Amer (Jaipur), who made common cause with Shivaji and encouraged him to accept a treaty and surrender to imperial authority as expediency in 1666. Savarkar quotes Shivaji's words of Hindu championship and martial resolve: "We are Hindus. The Mohammedans have subjugated the country and have defiled our sacred places! In fact they have desecrated our religion. We will therefore, protect our religion and for that we would even lose our lives. We will acquire new kingdoms by our prowess and that bread we will eat".

Periods of peace alternated with active hostilities, Maratha power increasing all the while. Continued successes involving the extortion of tribute from Mughal provinces enabled Shivaji to assume the dignity of an independent monarch "Chhatrapati", in a coronation at Raigarh in 1674. By the time of his passing, he had consolidated a small independent kingdom in western India. Although Shivaji's achievement, certainly rested on military prowess, his intense devotion to Hinduism was a vital factor in arousing the defiant nationalism of the Marathas against the Mughal power. He thus, welded his people of all castes into a new nation proud of its identity and Hindu religion.

Savarkar asserted that Maratha ascendancy was no parochial movement. He wrote: "The Hindu Empire was the great ideal which had fired the imagination and goaded the actions of Shivaji while he was but within his teens" and commented that "the rise of Hindu power under Shivaji had electrified the Hindu mind all over India. The oppressed looked upon him as an Avatar and a Saviour".

Savarkar traced the subsequent expansion of Maratha power across India in the reign of Baji Rao I and Balaji Baji Rao also known as Nana *saheb*. During the rule of the second *peshwa* Baji Rao (1740–1761), the Marathas became the masters of Gujarat, Malwa, and Bundelkhand and then invaded Delhi, the Mughal capital in 1737. The powerless and corrupt state of the Mughal Empire invited foreign intervention, first from the Persians in 1739, then from the Afghans. By 1758 the Marathas had occupied the Punjab and it seemed that they were destined to become the rulers of all India. Their frontier extended in the north to the River Indus and the Himalayas and in the south almost as far as the tip of the peninsula. Sadashiv Bhau, the cousin of the third *peshwa* Balaji Rao, was an outstanding military leader and the real power in the Maratha government. In 1760 he renewed the invasion of upper India and occupied Delhi, where the triumphant Marathas celebrated the eclipse of Mughal rule by hammering the imperial throne to pieces.

However, in January 1761 Maratha power suffered a huge reverse at the mighty third battle of Panipat outside Delhi against the Afghans, in which more than 200,000 Hindus and most Maratha leaders sacrificed their lives. But the Afghans gained no advantage; the losses suffered by Ahmed Shah Abdali, the victor of Panipat, paid to his dreams of ruling India; he could never return to this country again. The Mughal Empire was now defunct, and by 1771, within ten years of the Panipat disaster, the Marathas under another intrepid military leader Mahadji Scindia re-established their supremacy over northern India. Savarkar therefore, exalted the Marathas as the founders of a Hindu national state. In his view, this battle marked the definitive close of the Mughal period and left the Marathas, though significantly weakened, as the dominant regional power in India until the advent of the British Empire in 1818: "The day of Panipat rose, the Hindus lost the battle—and won the war. The triumphant Hindu banner that our Marathas had carried was taken up by our Sikhs. In this prolonged furious conflict our people became intensely conscious of ourselves as Hindus and were welded into a nation to an extent unknown in our history".

Following this review of the Maratha period as the era of pan-Hindu liberation, *Hindutva* was devoted to a description and celebration of Hinduness. Savarkar defined a Hindu as an Indian national, with references to the geographical unity of the subcontinent, the bonds of blood, and the maintenance of its purity by the caste system. "The Hindus are not merely the citizens of the Indian state," he asserted, "They are united not only by the bonds of love they bear to common motherland but also by the bonds of a common blood. All Hindus claim to have in their veins the blood of the mighty race incorporated with and descended from the Vedic fathers" and "No word can give a full expression to this racial unity of our people as the epithet Hindu does. We are all Hindus and own a common blood". However, besides their shared ancestry, Savarkar claimed that Hindus were culturally united by Hindu civilization through a common history, a common literature, a common art and architecture, a common law and jurisprudence, common fairs and festivals, rites and rituals, ceremonies and sacraments. India was not only a Hindu's fatherland but also his Holy Land, for it was the land of the Vedas, Hindu history and heroes.

Between 1924 and 1937 Savarkar was not permitted to leave the Ratnagiri district. Once this restriction was lifted, he resumed political activity, translating his philosophy of Hindutva into extreme Hindu nationalism. He was immediately elected president of the All India Hindu

Mahasabha at its nineteenth session held at Ahmedabad in 1937 and presided over its next five annual sessions. Although the Hindu Mahasabha had been founded as a social organisation in 1915, it now became a vigourous lobby group for Hindu interests under Savarkar's leadership. In his presidential speech of 1937, Savarkar described the Mahasabha as a pan-Hindu organisation with the task of "the maintenance, protection and promotion of the Hindu race, culture and civilization for the advance and glory of Hindu Rashtra... a national body representing the Hindu Nation as a whole", and keep a watchful eye on the anti-national designs of the Muslims in India.

At the twentieth session of the Hindu Mahasabha held at Nagpur in 1938, Savarkar attacked the Indian National Congress. In his view, its secular Indian patriotism had denied the Hinduness of the Indian majority while still failing to embrace the Muslims, who jealously defended their religious community and identity. The Congress was but a hostage of Muslim intransigence, constantly seeking to appease them to the disadvantage of the Hindu majority. Savarkar railed at the British for denying the Hindus political representation in proportion to their population through the Communal Award of 1932—in his view an unjust system of weightages and preferences—and for breaking up the Hindu electorate into such constituencies as to prevent the growth of Hindu political solidarity. He protested against the operation of quotas favouring Muslims in the government services (as high as 60 percent in Bengal, for example), and the curtailment of Hindu recruitment to the army and police with the result that the Muslim minority was predominant in these forces. Besides these political grievances, Savarkar drew attention to the plight of Hindus subjected to religious and racial persecution in the Muslim states of Hyderabad and Bhopal, and as the hapless victims of riots and tribal frontier raids. These grievances and the fear of permanent political subservience had indeed haunted the thinking and emotions of many Hindus throughout the 1930s.

Savarkar concluded that the Indian National Congress had failed the Hindus; its Indian patriotism was a secular sham, and only the Hindu Mahasabha could properly represent the Indian Hindu nation. Savarkar exhorted his followers to abandon the false ideas that had prevailed since the birth of the Congress in the 1880s. Hindu nationalism was the only effective form of Indian nationalism. After a brief review of the Maratha era of Hindu nationalism and the foundation of a Hindu empire, Savarkar demanded that the self-conscious Hindu nation must again be revived and resurrected. At the 1938 session of the Mahasabha, it was clear that Savarkar was advocating strident Hindu nationalism as the only effective response to Muslim provocation and growing hostility in national affairs.

A Greek lady who was devoted to the ancient Aryan culture and Hindu way of life had migrated to India and become a Hindu. She came to be known as Savitri Devi. She also went on to be closely associated with the Hindutva movement Savarkar and Hedgewar had set on the path of consolidation and revival of the Hindu nation. Her book *A Warning to the Hindus* (1939) was published under the auspices of the Hindu Mission where she had worked for some eighteen months. The book was evidently highly regarded by the mission, for it was also published in six Indian languages, including Bengali, Hindi, and Marathi. The first chapter, "Indian Nationalism and Hindu Consciousness" echoes V D Savarkar's rallying cry of

Hindutva with her main thesis that Hinduism is the national religion of India and that there is no real India besides Hindu India. She was similarly contemptuous of Congress's secular patriotism and asserted that, "there is no such thing as an Indian civilization which is neither Hindu nor Musulman. The only civilization for all India is Hindu civilization. The only culture for all India is Hindu culture. Indian national consciousness is nothing else but Hindu national consciousness." And again, "As nothing is more necessary to India, today, than a strong national consciousness and national pride; nothing is more necessary, today, than to revive, to exalt, to cultivate intelligent Hinduism through the length and breadth of India".

Her work at the Hindu Mission had familiarised her with the grievances of Hindus and their sense of embattlement in the increasingly Muslim culture of some provinces. In a chapter "The Defence of Hindudom: A Danger Signal," she produced statistics on the relative numerical strengths of Hindus and Muslims in various Indian states. She conceded that the Muslim minority was still negligible in the Far South (3 per cent), Orisha (2 percent), Bihar (10 percent), the United Provinces (13 per cent), the Central Provinces (5 per cent) and West Bengal (6 per cent). However, on turning her attention to the Punjab, "the cradle of Aryan culture in India," and Bengal, her own adopted province, she saw cause for grave concern. Estimating the Hindu population of Bengal at 22 million and the Muslim population at 28 million, with a further 2 million in the border district of Assam, she found that the Muslim population of Bengal was practically half the entire Muslim population of British India. She commented that this Muslim population of Bengal alone was already more than double that of Turkey and that the

Muslim population of just one of the Bengal's districts (Mymen singh) was more than half that of all Arabia.

Savitri Devi argued that it was not the tenets of Hinduism that were in danger; they would always hold true irrespective of the numbers of Hindus. It was the Hindus as a nation who were in danger of extinction, at least in some parts of India. She defended Hindudom more than the Hindu religion. She recalled that the truth in Plato's writings was still true, but that it did not prevent ancient Greek society and civilization from passing away. Similarly, "The value of Hinduism will not save Hindudom, if it is not strong, numerically and politically".

Savitri Devi saw ominous parallels between the fate of pagan classical Greece and the endangered Hindudom of India. She compared the experience of beleaguered Hindus in Muslim-dominated provinces to that of Greek pagans in their own country during the early Middle Ages. She recalled the oppression of the last pagans by the Christians: works of art destroyed, festivities stopped, schools of philosophy shut down, wise men exiled. She characterised the period from Emperor Constantine I until the accession of Emperor Julian (331–363 AD) in terms of "the growing tyranny exercised by the Christians upon the declining minority of Pagans, in the towns and villages of Greece, Asia-Minor, Egypt and Italy".

This alarmist comparison between ancient Greece and present day India could be extended to indicate the dreadful possibility that Hindu India might itself become a dead civilization. In the context of a threatened Hindu world, Savitri's memories of the sun-bleached ruins of Athens and the Attic peninsula were no longer just relics of a golden age but omens for India: "Greece is covered with gorgeous ruins. Upon steep promontories, there are still rows of white columns, looking over the blue sea, full of isles. There are blocks of sculptured marble, and old statues to be found even in the market place. But living life all around, runs on different lines. The national gods have become objects of admiration in museums. But nobody worships them. There are no Panathenian processions, in pomp and glory, going up the Acropolis today".

She warned that Hindu complacency and inaction were a clear sign of weakness, that Hindudom was yielding every day to hostile forces, losing its numerical advantage, its political rights in the country, and its place as a nation. The fate of pagan Greece could easily overtake the Hindus and become the fate of pagan India tomorrow. She painted a desolate picture of India without Hindus: "A swarm of mosques will be built here and there, in the place of minor shrines. Mohammedan life and European life combined will make unrecognizable India look much like modern Egypt. Cultured Indians will look upon their national gods as Christian Europeans look upon Greek 'mythology'. And the Ganges will still be flowing. But there will be no ritual bathing in its waters, no pilgrims going up and down its *ghats*, no garlands of flowers thrown into it as an offering. India will no longer be 'our' India".

Savitri Devi followed the Hindu nationalists in her recommendation of measures for a revival of Hindudom. In her chapter devoted to social reforms, she identified the major causes of numerical losses in Hindudom as the denial of elementary social rights to the minority of Hindus; the strictness of social rules within the Hindu fold, leading to the easy outcasting of transgressors; and the refusal of the Hindu fold to accept those who wished to return, let alone those who wanted to convert to Hinduism. Again, she drew a parallel with the ancient world. The triumph of Christianity was largely attributable to the rigidity of the Greeco-Roman social order. Although ancient Greek and Roman society were not as complicated and caste-ridden as Hindudom, there was a wide gulf between the free man and the slave.

The universal appeal of Christianity to all men exploded such division and hierarchy. Savitri echoed the fierce anti-Christian invective of Friedrich Nietzsche (1844–1900), regarding the victory of Christianity as a widespread revolt of the slaves and barbarians against the existing social order of the Roman Empire. Mindful of this historical failure in Europe, She advised the relaxation of the caste system with its rights and privileges, in order to develop a Hindu populism. Here she was reflecting the ideas of V D Savarkar, who too regarded the caste system as a brake on the development of Hindu solidarity and nationalism.

Some upper-caste Hindus were prone to cling on to their rights and exclusiveness but what good could such regressive attitudes achieve if everything was swept away if the Hindu way of life were to suffer extinction. History stands witness to the reality that the noble families of ancient Greece and Rome were lost. No single modern Greek or Roman can today be sure that there are neither slaves nor barbarians among his/her ancestors. Their defence of family privilege could not address the universal challenge of Christianity and, in consequence, the vigour and endurance of the old pre-Christian culture of Europe was lost. Unless the Hindus now make a mighty effort to overcome the disadvantages of Hindu society, there may be no future for all Hindus, let alone for the precious privileges of the Hindu elite.

Dr Balkrishna Shivram Moonje, later president of the Hindu Mahasabha, was also co-founder of the RSS, and Ganesh Savarkar, Vinayak's brother, helped the organisation expand in western Maharashtra by merging his own Tarun Hindu Sabha (Hindu Youth) and Mukteshwar Dal (Liberation Organisation) into the RSS. In 1927, Hedgewar instituted the Officers' Training Camp (OTC) in order to build a corps of *pracharaks* (preachers), who formed the leadership of the RSS. Celibate and leading an austere life of devotion to the cause (even today), members of this elite group acted as military-group leaders and gurus to the young Hindu men. Lacking trained cadres of its own, the Hindu Mahasabha regarded the RSS as a valuable asset for youth politics. At its 1932 Delhi session the Mahasabha commended its activities and emphasised the need to spread its network all over the country. The RSS *shakha* (local branch) network expanded from 18 in the Nagpur region in 1928 to about 125 (with 12,000 volunteers) throughout Maharashtra in 1933. By the late 1930s, with sharpening Hindu-Muslim conflict in North India, the RSS had covered many provinces with some 40,000 volunteers in 400 *shakhas* in 1938, rising to 60,000 in 500 branches by 1939.

Nehru and his ideological fellow-travellers saw the RSS as an Indian version of fascism. By the late 1930s the Hindu nationalists were taking note of European fascism. Savarkar approved the German occupation of the Sudetenland on the grounds of common blood, and the Nazi Party paper, the *Volkischer Beobachter*, carried a feature on him. When Madhav Sadashiv Golwalkar, shortly to succeed Hedgewar as RSS leader, published his book *We, or Our Nationhood Defined* (1939), the RSS message of ethnic nationalism was unequivocal. Golwalkar rejected Congress's liberal concept of nationhood.

In contrast to his mentor Hedgewar, Golwalkar advocated a strongly racial concept of the Hindu nation and urged Hindus to regard themselves at war with both the Muslims and the British. The RSS went on to become the crucible of Hindu national identity.

The year 1939 had seen massive demonstrations of Hindu nationalists in the Muslim Nizam state of Hyderabad. This civil resistance movement against the Nizam led by the Arya Samaj and the Hindu Mahasabha fielded more than fifteen thousand supporters. Punjabis, Madrasis, Sindhis, Bengalis, Beharis, Marathas, Sikhs, Jains, Brahmins, and Bhangis, rich and poor, the Hindus joined in marches and protests for a six-month period under a common Hindu banner. The orange pan-Hindu Mahasabha flag with its immemorial Vedic symbols of green swastika, lotus stem, and curved sword beneath the holy word *OM* flew triumphantly over the massed ranks of demonstrators throughout the Nizam state. Savarkar saw the movement as a Hindu crusade and paid a fulsome tribute to all participants in his presidential address to the Mahasabha later that year.

Following Indian's independence in 1947, the RSS with about 600,000 volunteers nationwide entered national politics. Briefly banned after Gandhi's assassination, Golwalkar's RSS network launched a new party—the Bharatiya Jana Sangh in 1951, which became the Bharatiya Janata Party (BJP) in 1980. In the early 1990s, with Muslim confrontation and the bid to restore Hindu authority, the BJP re-enacted the urgency of the situation in the 1930s. New plans for a magnificent Rama temple in the holy city of Ayodhya were mooted. The demolition of the Babri Masjid mosque on the proposed site by Hindutva activists on 6 December 1992, an image flashed worldwide by news agencies, was but another climax in the long history of

Hindutva politics. Finally, after more than two decades of political see-saws and legal entanglements, construction of the proposed temple to Rama commenced on May 26 2020 at Ayodhya, befittingly under a BJP government led by the chief minister who by vocation is a Hindu monk belonging to the Gorakhnath Pitha, a mystic order of many millennia ago.

6

Violence and Hindudom

Is Hindudom uncomfortable with violence or is it unafraid to engage with it, when the need arises? It is imperative that we seek answers to this. The leading figure of India's freedom movement from British colonial rule was MK Gandhi, who is widely revered as Mahatma Gandhi around the world. Gandhi is worshipped as the foremost avatar of *ahimsa* or non-violence as any kind of violent action or reaction towards even enemies was anathema to him. Ironically, it was Gandhi's vehement insistence that Hindus exercise total non-violence against Muslims even after suffering genocide at the latter's hands in the brutal aftermath of Partition that led to a Hindu backlash, culminating in the latter's assassination at the hands of Nathuram Godse.

Even more ironical would be to associate Gandhi with an instrument of state force, for example, policing. But it was also said of this apostle of non-violence: "Gandhi is the best policeman we have in India." This was stated by Ellen Wilkinson, Member of Parliament (Labour Party) in 1932 after a visit to India. There was terrorism over the turn of the 19th into the 20th century that went on well into the

1920s. Then Gandhi took over the reins of the Congress Party and terrorism happened to fade out. There were incidents of violence like the setting fire to the police station at Chauri Chaura in Uttar Pradesh, upon which Gandhi called off his *satyagraha* of the Non-co-operation movement. He could not tolerate the heinous act of violence. Dr BR Ambedkar was candid when he wrote that between 1920 and 1940, there was a virtual civil war between Hindus and Muslims. There were numerous communal riots, but few attacks on British officers.

Coming to violence, Gandhi complimented Muslims again and again. When they raped, converted and killed thousands of Hindus in the Moplah riots in Malabar (northern Kerala) in 1921, his cold comment was that the Muslims had only followed their religion. When one Abdul Rashid murdered Swami Shraddhanand an Arya Samaj missionary, in December 1926, Gandhi called the killer his brother. The British government tried Rashid forthwith and hanged him to death. Muslims, on the contrary, did not show appreciation or deference for Gandhi's kindness. For example, Maulana Muhammad Ali, the Khilafat leader, said openly that *momins* (the faithful of Islam) would care more for a fallen Muslim than for the non-Muslim Gandhi; this was a demonstration of unprovoked contempt. Yet, such endorsement of violence by non-Hindus would evoke not even protest, let alone opposition from the apostle of ahimsa.

There are no two opinions that non-violence is much preferable to violence; provided of course, it can deliver what is essential. In many ways, Jainism personifies the essence of Hinduism which wishes to avoid hurting or causing pain to any living being as far as possible.

The two atom bombs that fell on Hiroshima and Nagasaki in August 1945 revealed to the world that a great new deterrent to large scale violence had been born. As, in course of time, other countries made nuclear weapons, the deterrence grew and spread. The Cold War between USA and Soviet-Union was fought, won and lost without firing a bullet. Vicariously, this was a victory for the Hindu view that even a mega war can be fought without shedding blood.

But beyond a point, Hindus need not gloat with delight over this historic development. There is a simple reason for this; the flipside of violence is not non-violence in statecraft. Incidentally, Gandhi had no exposure to governance; his forte was agitation. The flipside is an unchanged degree of the will to fight as well as the discovery of a variety of methods of fighting that do not require firing bullets. In order to wage a war, one need not fire bullets, shells, bombs or missiles as proved by the Cold War. President Ronald Reagan of the USA unleashed an idea of "Star Wars", which involved building a giant network of laser beams to destroy incoming Soviet ballistic nuclear missiles. Reagan's idea was part of his strategy of destroying the communist adversary without firing a shot. The grossly inefficient Soviet Union could not keep pace, and if it tried to do so, its hollow economy would go bust, as it eventually did. Along with the Soviet economy, the Soviet Union itself broke up and scattered into history.

Such a novel strategy does not need only raw brawn but a great deal of brainpower and, above all, an extra-ordinary will to fight and overwhelm the adversary. The Hindu deficiency during the medieval centuries (13th to the 18th) was, in most parts of the country, a lack of will to fight at most times. Soldiers, generals and weapons could be raised provided there was a determination to defeat and drive out the invaders.

It is no one's case that Hindus do not have brawn or brainpower. A significant number of Mughal generals were Hindu, on whom the empire depended for its aggrandizement and at times, its very survival. For example, Akbar fielded Raja Man Singh of Jaipur against Maharana Pratap at the Battle of Haldighati. Mirza Raja Jai Singh was the most effective general of Aurangzeb; the latter's bigotry had to accept the indispensability of the *kafir* Rajput. What was lacking was the Rajput will to try and overturn the invaders. For example, Hemchandra Vikramaditya nearly defeated Akbar and his uncle Bairam Khan at the Second Battle of Panipat on 5 November 1556. Had a freak arrow not pierced Hemu's eye, there could have been a Hindu on the throne of Delhi for the first time since Prithviraj Chauhan in 1192 AD. Hemu had the will to fight apart from other skills.

An example of pure Hindu brain and will was demonstrated by Raja Nabakrishna Deb and Jagat Seth in 1756-1757. When they came to know that the directors of the East India Company in London had asked that Robert Clive and an Admiral be sent to Bengal they hit upon an idea. They saw in this opportunity the chance of history, not merely of a lifetime. Bengal was possibly the most prosperous *subah* (province) of the Mughal Empire which had devolved to Nawab Ali Vardi Khan. Whatever might have been his efficacy as a ruler, there was no mistaking his religious bias. Nevertheless, Bengal was a large *subah* extending well into Bihar and Odisha as well. Today's Bangladesh was also an integral part of it. There were several merchant princes, mostly Hindus, who had a greater knack for business than the Muslims whose wealth was largely land-based. Nawab Ali Vardi was succeeded by his daughter's son Siraj-ud-Dawla, a brash and immature young man. The merchant princes felt that he would ruin Bengal and therefore, ought to be removed. The Hindus of Bengal lacked the power or confidence to do so on their own; Robert Clive's arrival was thus, a golden opportunity. Helping the incoming Englishman, therefore, became their plan.

With the resources at their disposal, they were able to inveigle Mir Jafar, Nawab Siraj-ud-Dawla's chief commander, to not fight but defect on the day of the battle. If he kept his word, the merchant princes would ensure that he would be made the Nawab of Bengal after the current young ruler was disposed of. On 23June 1757, the battle opened near the village of Plassey not far from Murshidabad. Siraj's army numbered about one lakh men whereas Clive had no more than 3,000 soldiers and sepoys at his disposal, but by evening the latter had decisively won the day. The Battle of Plassey was the first defeat and disposal of a major Muslim ruler in many years. Admittedly, the victory was not of the Hindus but their intrigue had succeeded in toppling the Muslim rulers of eastern India from their throne. The Hindus had achieved a level playing field in the east. Symbolic of this achievement was that later in the year 1757, the Durga Puja, so close to the heart and psyche of the Bengali, was celebrated publicly for the first time in memory. Until then the puja had to be behind closed doors out of fear of attracting the adverse attention of the Nawabi ruling class and its followers. Incidentally, Robert Clive was the chief guest at this celebration at the palatial bungalow of Raja Nabakrishna Deb, the leading merchant prince.

While the Raja or his associates, Jagat Seth and others, could not mobilise an army to fight the nawab, they at least displayed a will to fight and to get the East India Company to fight their war. The old saying "where there is a will, there is a way" was proved and it turned out to be a very skilful way. In 1799, Lord Wellesley defeated and disposed of Tipu Sultan; thus, the deep south of India was also cleared of nawabi rule. Lord Dalhousie, in 1856, took over Nawab Wajid Ali Shah and his state of Awadh in north India. The next in the series of events was the Great Rebellion, which the British called the Sepoy Mutiny of 1857-1858. Queen Victoria took over the whole of India thus, ending what was the proud Dar-ul-Islam, (land of Islam), of the Muslims in India. The will and the wile displayed by the merchant princes of Bengal in 1757 saw the whole sub-continent turn into Dar-ul-Harb or the land of conflict (for Muslims). Ideally, it should have been "Dar-ul-Hindu" but regrettably, the Hindus had neither national unity nor a tall enough leader who could have achieved it.

This brings us to the question of unity. Against Mohammed Ghori at the end of the 12th century, King Jaichand of Kannauj did not go to the support of Prithviraj Chauhan. Had he done so, Ghori would certainly have been defeated and the Sultanate would not have been established in Delhi in 1206. In that case, possibly the medieval history of India might have been different. Hindu civilization would then have continued in all its glory. The same Chauhans of Ajmer and Delhi had neglected their responsibility towards Hindu unity only a few years earlier in 1178 AD, when they did not go to the aid of the Solankis (Bhola Bhimdev II) of Gujarat against the same Ghori. Fortunately, the Turk was defeated by the Solankis, and sent packing from Gujarat. The great Hindu hero Maharana Pratap had to fight by himself to save his Mewar. No other prince came to his support against Akbar, who incidentally was served by dozens of Hindu princes. Chhatrapati Shivaji had worked wonders which could have been followed up by the Marathas replacing the moribund Mughals in Delhi. They, however, could not remain united; instead they scattered into five separate kingdoms. Ironically, the ruler of Gwalior paid the Mughal emperor a pension for some years but did not replace him. What can explain this shortcoming in the Hindu character?

The karma of Hindu is individual and its reward or punishment comes to the individual. It probably does not occur to him or her that working in unison with others is necessarily a desirable karma or a *punya.* In contrast, the Abrahamic faiths, Judaism, Christianity or Islam, believe in their respective God who shall deliver His judgement on the faithful on doomsday. The performance of the faithful would have a great deal to do with society, or his/her fellow beings. For example, one sees the Christian commitment to social service, hospitals and schools. Islam insists on the payment of *zakat* of two and a half percent by every well-to-do Muslim of his wealth every year. The money thus, collected is spent on the welfare of the poor and the needy. The judgement of God is all-important; there is no belief in the automatic consequence of karma and its resultant *bhagya* or fate.

Gandhi, by himself, was a specimen of disunity. He dressed like a Hindu, loved listening to *bhajans* or songs to remember the divine. His idiom of expressions was Hindu. But when the Muslims slaughtered Hindus in Malabar his only response was that "they were practicing their religion" (quote from article written by Gandhi in *Young India*, October 1921). When Hindus in Kohat, Baluchistan, suffered at the hands of Muslims in the riots of 1924, Gandhi advised the Hindus to show their bravery by getting killed and exhorted them not to flee the area. Earlier he had assumed the presidentship of the Khilafat Committee whose sole objective was to persuade the British to allow the Caliph to survive on the Turkish throne. How was he, a Hindu, supposed to be concerned with the revival of an obscurantist medieval Islamic sultanate was something only he could know. Even Mohammed Ali Jinnah did not support the Khilafat Movement. Do not all these reactions of the great man reflect that he was a political schizophrenic?

It is natural in a free society for people, especially the educated, to range in their views, from the extremist or hard-line to the moderate or to the liberal. But why should so many Hindus call themselves secular only to be critical of their faith, to the extent of being anti-Hindu? It is difficult to think of another faith which can be so critical of itself. At the same time, the average Hindu is so believing and faithful and their numbers are increasing whether in the cities or the villages. This paradox does need explaining.

The Hindu has long belonged to a culture that prefers to speak and listen (*vakta and shrota*) rather than write and read. Ancient India might not have been like that but then in those old centuries, the educational and the intellectual functions were largely the monopoly of the elite. Evidently, circumstances then were different. With the advent of the British, English increasingly became the language of higher education, which tended to cut out the masses as well as students in mofussils and villages. As a result, literature in English on Hindu culture with its political corollaries was scarce. The buyers for such literature were also comparatively few. In short, the market was confined largely to the Sangh Parivar. An urgent and additional factor was the assassination of Gandhi, which had caused a revulsion amongst many Indians, although by 1946, his political image was declining. Even Vallabhbhai Patel and Jawaharlal Nehru had begun paying less and less heed to what Gandhi said.

The assassination reversed this trend and thereafter, for years in popular eyes, Gandhi became as great and glorious as he ever was. In fact, electorally, the Hindu parties lost up to 40 years in their prospects.

The election of Atal Bihari Vajpayee as prime minister in the late 1990s was a signal that sentiments were returning to normal. The effects of this Hindu revulsion at Gandhi's killing had been such that even Hindu leaders shied away from publicly acknowledging their faith. For example, Lal Krishna Advani, from being a respected party *apparatchik* (official), was catapulted to the position of a national leader by his *rathyatra* from Somnath to Ayodhya (interrupted by his arrest at Samastipur). His political cradle was the RSS and yet, he had no hesitation in disassociating himself from the Ram Janmabhoomi cause because he began perceiving Hindutva to be politically embarrassing. Murli Manohar Joshi, again a top flank leader, also followed the same path. Atal Bihari Vajpayee was an inveterate liberal, who incidentally was the biggest beneficiary of the non-Hindu environment resulting from Gandhi's assassination.

I, at the turn of this century happened to write four books—*The Saffron Book*, *Hindu Masjids*, *Population Exchange* and *Anti-Hindus*. Not only could I not find a publisher, bookshops too were reluctant to stock these books. In Bareilly, a bookshop owner was attracted to *Hindu Masjids* and promptly bought one copy. He said he would take it home and savour it, but dared not stock any copies for sale, lest somebody set fire to his shop. Such was the environment ridden with fear. What market for Hindu books could it sustain?

Consequently, someone deeply interested in politics would be able to read about every ideology except Hindu politics. The Indian language market was better, but not a great deal. Most of those who read political literature became followers of ideologies other than Hindu. Perhaps the reluctance to commit violence, not necessarily bloodshed, but the will to fight and overwhelm, embedded in the Hindu psyche might be the reason.

7

Nature's Unique Blessing to Hindustan (VD Savarkar)

It will not be out of place to see how far the attributes, which we found to be the essentials of Hindutva, contribute towards the strength, cohesion and progress of our people. Do these essentials constitute a foundation so broad, so deep and so strong that based on it the Hindu people can build a future which can face and repel the attacks of all the adverse winds that blow; or does the Hindu race stand on feet of clay?

Some of the ancient nations raised huge walls so as to convert a whole country into a fortified castle. Today their walls are trodden to dust or are but scarcely discernible by a few scattered mounds here and there, while the people they were meant to protect are not discernible at all. Our ancient neighbours, the Chinese, laboured from generation to generation and raised a rampart embracing the limits of an empire—so wide, so high—so strong—a wonder of the human world. But behold the ramparts of Nature! Have they not, these Himalayas, been standing there as one whose desires are satisfied—so they seemed to the Vedic bards—so they seem to us today. These are our ramparts that have converted this vast continent into a cosy castle.

You take up buckets and fill your trenches with water and call it a moat. Behold Varuna himself, with his one hand pushing continents aside, fills the gap by pouring in seas! This Indian Ocean with its bays and gulfs is our moat. These are our frontier lines within our reach—the advantages of an island as well as an insular country.

She is the richly endowed daughter of God—this Motherland. Her rivers are deep and perennial. Her land is yielding to the plough and her fields loaded with golden harvests. Her necessaries of life are few and a genial nature yields them all almost for the asking. Rich in her fauna, rich in her flora, she knows she owes it all to the immediate source of light and heat—the sun. She covets not the icy lands; blessed be they and their frozen latitudes. If heat is at times enervating here, cold is at times benumbing there. If cold induces manual labour, heat removes much of its very necessity. She takes more delight in quenched thirst than in the parched throat. Those who have not, let them delight in exerting to have. But those who have may be allowed to derive pleasure from the very fact of having. Father Thames is free to work at feverish speed, wrapped in his icy sheets. She loves to visit her ghats and watch her boats gliding down the Ganges on her moonlit waters. With the plough, the peacocks, and lotus, the elephant and the Gita, she is willing to forego, if that must be, whatever advantage the colder latitudes enjoy. She knows she cannot have all her own way. Her gardens are green and shady, her granaries well-stocked, her waters crystal, her flowers scented, her fruits juicy and her herbs healing. Her brush is dipped in the colours of dawn and her flute resonant with the music of Gokul. Verily, Hind is the richly endowed daughter of God.

Neither the English nor the French—with the exception of the Chinese and perhaps the Americans—no people are gifted with a land that can equal in natural strength and richness the land of Hindhustan. A country, a common home is the first important essential of a stable strong nationality; of all countries in the world our country can hardly be surpassed by any in its capacity to afford a soil so specially fitted for the growth of a great nation. We Hindus, whose very first article of faith is the love we bear to the common—Fatherland, have in that love the strongest talismanic tie that can bind close and keep a nation firm, and enthuse and enable it to accomplish things greater than ever.

The second essential of Hindutva puts the estimate of our latent powers of national cohesion and greatness yet higher. No country in the world with the exception of China again, is peopled by a race so homogeneous, yet so ancient and so strong both numerically and vitally. The Americans, too, whom we find equally fortunate as us so far as excellent geographical basis of nationality is concerned, are decidedly left behind. Mohammedans are no race nor are the Christians. They are a religious unit, yet neither a racial nor a national one. But we Hindus, if possible, are all the three put together, and live under our ancient and common roof. The numerical strength of our race is an asset that cannot be too highly prized.

And culture? The English and the Americans feel they are kith and kin because they possess a Shakespeare in common. But not only Kalidas or a Bhasa but, Oh Hindus! Ye possess a *Ramayana* and *Mahabharata* in common—and the Vedas! One of the national songs the American children are taught to sing attempts to rouse their sense of eternal self-importance by pointing out to the hundred years that stand behind their history. The Hindu counts his years not by centuries but by cycles—the Yuga and the Kalpa.

The Uttar Kosala of Raghupathi is nowhere to be seen, nor is Shri Krishna's city of Mathura.

The Hindu does not attempt to rouse the sense of self-importance so much as the sense of proportion which is Truth. And that has perhaps made him last longer than Rameses and Nebuchadnezzar. A people that had produced an unending galaxy of heroes and hero-worshippers and who are conscious of having fought with and vanquished the forces whose might struck Greece and Rome, the Pharaohs and the Incas, dead, have in their history a guarantee of their future greatness more assuring than any other people on earth yet possess.

But besides culture, the tie of a common holy land has at times proved stronger than the chains of a Motherland. Look at the Mohammedans. Mecca to them is a sterner reality than Delhi or Agra. Some of them do not make any secret of being bound to sacrifice all of India if that be to the glory of Islam or could save the city of their prophet. Look at the Jews; neither centuries of prosperity nor sense of gratitude for the shelter they found, can make them more attached or even equally attached to the several countries they inhabit. Their love is, and must necessarily be divided between the land of their birth and the land of their Prophets. If the Zionists' dreams are ever realised—if Palestine becomes a Jewish State, and it will gladden us almost as much as our Jewish friends—they, like the Mohammedans would naturally set the interests of their Holy Land above those of their Motherland in America and Europe and in case of war between their adopted country and the Jewish State, would naturally sympathise with the latter, if indeed they do not bodily go over to it. History is too full of examples of such desertions to cite particulars. The Crusades too, attest to the wonderful influence that a common holy land exercises over people widely separated in race, nationality and language, to bind and hold them together.

The ideal conditions, therefore, under which a nation can attain perfect solidarity and cohesion would, other things being equal, be found in the case of those people who inhabit the land they adore, the land of whose forefathers is also the land of their gods and angels, of seers and prophets; the scenes of whose history are also the scenes of their mythology.

The Hindus are about the only people who are blessed with these ideal conditions that are at the same time an incentive to national solidarity, cohesion and greatness. Not even the Chinese are blessed. Only Arabia and Palestine, if ever the Jews can succeed in founding their state there, can be said to possess this unique advantage. But Arabia is incomparably poorer in the natural, cultural, historical, and numerical essentials of a great people; and even if the dreams of the Zionists are ever realise into a Palestine State, still they too must be equally lacking in these.

England, France, Germany, Italy, Turkey proper, Persia, Japan, Afghanistan, Egypt of today (for the old descendants of Punta and their Egypt is dead long since), and other African states, Mexico, Peru, Chile (not to mention states and nations lesser than all these), though racially more or less homogeneous are yet less advantageously situated than we are in geographical, cultural, historical and numerical essentials, besides lacking the unique gift of a sanctified

Motherland. Of the remaining nations, Russia in Europe, and the United States of America, though geographically equally well-gifted as us, are yet poorer in almost every other requisite of nationality. China alone of the present comity of nations is almost as richly gifted with the geographical, racial, cultural essentials as the Hindus are. Only in the possession of a common, a sacred and a perfect language, Sanskrit, and a sanctified Motherland, we are, so far as the essentials that contribute to national solidarity are concerned, more fortunate.

Thus, the actual essentials of Hindutva are, as this running sketch reveals, also the ideal essentials of nationality. If we want, we could build on this foundation of Hindutva a future greater than what any other people on earth can dream of, greater even than our own past; provided we are able to utilise our opportunities. For let our people remember that great combinations are the order of the day. The League of Nations, the alliances of powers, Pan-Islamism, Pan-Slavism, Pan-Ethoiopism, all little beings are seeking to get themselves incorporated into greater wholes, so as to be better fitted for the struggle for existence and power. Those who are not naturally and historically blessed with numerical or geographical or racial advantages are seeking to share them with others. Woe to those who have them already as their birthright and know them not; or worse, despise them! The nations of the world are desperately trying to find a place in this or that combination for aggression—can anyone of you, Oh Hindus, whether Jain or Samaji or Sanatani or Sikh or any other sub-section, afford to cut yourselves off or fall out and destroy the ancient, the natural and the organic combination that already exists?—a combination that is bound not by any scraps of paper nor by the ties of exigencies alone, but by the ties of blood, birth and culture? Strengthen them if you can: pull down the barriers that have survived their utility, of castes and customs, of sects and sections. Intermarriages between provinces and provinces, castes and castes must be encouraged where they do not exist. But where they already exist as between the Sikhs and Sanatanis, Jain and Vaishnavas, Lingayats and Non-Lingayats—suicidal be the hand that tries to cut the nuptial tie. Let the minorities remember they would be cutting the very branch on which they sit. Strengthen every tie that binds you to the main organism, whether of blood or language or common Motherland. Let this ancient and noble stream of Hindu blood flow from vein to vein, from Attock to Cuttack till at last the Hindu people get fused and welded into an indivisible whole, till our race gets consolidated and strong, sharp as steel.

Just cast a glance at the past, then at the Pan-Islamism in Asia, the political language in Europe, the Pan-Ethiopic movement in Africa and America—and then see, O Hindus, if your future is not entirely bound up with the future of India and the future of India is bound up in the last resort, with Hindu strength. We are trying our best, as we ought to do, to develop the consciousness of and a sense of attachment to the greater whole, whereby Hindus, Mohammedans, Parsis, Christians and Jews would feel as Indians first and every other thing afterwards. But whatever progress India may have made to that goal, one thing remains almost axiomatically true—not only in India but everywhere in the world—that a nation requires a foundation to stand upon, and the essence of the life of a nation is the life of that portion of its citizens whose interest and history and aspirations are most closely bound up with the land and who thus, provide the real foundation to the structure of their national state. Take the case of Turkey. The young

Turks after the revolution had to open their Parliament and military institutions to Armenians and Christians on a non-religious and secular basis. But when the war with Serbia came, the Christians and Armenians first wavered and then many a regiment consisting of them went bodily over to the Serbians, who politically and racially and religiously were more closely bound up with them. Take the case of America. When the German war broke out she suddenly had to face the danger of desertions of her German citizens, while the Negro citizens there sympathise more with their brethren in Africa than with their white countryman. The American State, in the last resort, must stand or fall with the fortunes of its Anglo-Saxon constituents. So with the Hindus. They being the people, whose past, present and future are most closely bound with the soil of Hindustan as *Pitribhu* (Fatherland), as *Punyabhu* (Holy Land), they constitute the foundation, the bedrock, the reserved forces of the Indian state. Therefore, even from the point of Indian nationality, must ye, O Hindus, consolidate and strengthen Hindu nationality; not to give wanton offence to any of our non-Hindu compatriots, in fact to anyone in the world, but in just and urgent defence of our race and land; to render it impossible for others to betray her or to subject her to unprovoked attack by any of those 'Pan-isms' that are struggling forth from continent to continent. As long as other communities in India or the world are not respectively planning India first or mankind first, but all are busy in organizing offensive and defensive alliances and combinations on entirely narrow racial or religious or national basis, so long, at least, O Hindus, strengthen if you can those subtle bonds that like nerve threads bind you in one organic social being. Those of you who in a suicidal fit try to cut off the most vital of those ties and dare to disown the name Hindu will find to their cost that in doing so they have cut themselves off from the very source of our racial life and strength.

The presence of only a few of these essentials of nationality which we have found to constitute Hindutva enabled little nations like Spain or Portugal to get themselves lionized in the world. But when all of those ideal conditions obtain here, what is there in the human world that the Hindus cannot accomplish?

Thirty crores of people, with India for their basis of operation, for their Fatherland and Holy Land, with such a history behind them, bound together by ties of a common blood and common culture can dictate their terms to the whole world. A day will come when mankind will have to face this force.

Equally certain it is that whenever the Hindus come to hold such a position whence they could dictate terms to the whole world—those terms cannot be very different from the terms which Gita dictates or the Buddha lays down. A Hindu is most intensely so, when he ceases to be a Hindu; and with a Shankar claims the whole earth for a Banaras 'Varanasi Medini!' or with a Tukaram exclaims: My country? Oh brothers, the limits of the Universe—there the frontiers of my country lie.

(From Veer Savarkar's book *Hindutva*).

8

Tolerance

In the view of many, Hindus do not unite against an enemy as spontaneously as some other communities. If this is true, it is illustrated by a well-known legend millennia ago. A *dasyu* (dacoit), Ratnakar, was reputed to play havoc with innocent passers-by not very far from Ayodhya. One such traveller, the celestial sage Narada, was cornered by Ratnakar. The sage declared he had nothing but his *veena*, the musical instrument on whose strings he continually played a tune while chanting the name of Lord Narayana (Vishnu).

"What do you do with the wealth you collect and the little animals you kill?" asked Narada of the dacoit. Ratnakar's proud answer was that he would take it all home and share it with his family—his wife, children and parents. The dacoit added that this endeavour was for all of them. In return, the sage remarked that Ratnakar looted or/and killed, while all his family enjoyed his ill-gotten gains; but he questioned whether they were ready to share the *durbhagya* or the ill fate, i.e., punishment for his *dushkarma* (bad deeds) of plunder and murder. Were they all prepared to suffer divine punishment for his sins?

Perceiving he had confounded Ratnakar, Narada asked him to go home and ask his family if he himself didn't know the answer. Would they share the suffering as they did the pleasures he brought home? And so Ratnakar the robber went home to ask each one of his dear ones. Their candid reply was: "Why should they?" They knew little about where the goodies came from. They presumed they were Ratnakar's earnings. Crestfallen, he went back to where Narada was waiting in the forest. He wept as he confessed his folly to the sage.

Narada asked Ratnakar to stop crying for that wouldn't help, but start chanting the name of Rama continually. His penance and meditation took years, during which a *valmik* or anthill gradually formed around his motionless body. When the robber-turned-pious individual finally emerged from the *valmik*, he had become the sage Valmiki, who went on to write about the life and doings of Rama, which is the *Ramayana*. That was how Ratnakar turned Valmiki began writing the *Ramayana*. And possibly Hindus became circumspect about leaping before looking at the actions of others.

Hindus are widely recognised as tolerant people, especially in their attitude towards members of other faiths. Jews are likely to swear that the land of the Hindus is one land where they have never been discriminated against or persecuted. Their experience in Christian countries has been tragic, they say, and perhaps elsewhere as well. The life of Parsis in India has been a happy one since they came here seeking refuge from Islamic persecution in Iran. Ever since they landed at Sanjan in the South of Gujarat over a millennium ago they have been, as a community, happy and prosperous. They have enjoyed complete freedom of worship. So have members of other religions. Unfortunately, not all have reciprocated this tolerance. Islam has been frequently occupied in conquest, domination and often oppression. Christianity's preoccupation has been with conversion of Hindus to the faith of Jesus Christ, although the community's contribution to education and health has been laudable.

These faiths are upheld by the declaration that a particular entity is their god; they follow a particular book or books that will tell them the dos and don'ts of the religion. Up to a point, the follower may raise questions but beyond a limit, it will begin to become apostasy. These faiths are organised with a hierarchy of priests or other learned persons to guide the followers as well as to manage the faith. Once well set, these faiths are easy for everyone to follow.

These faiths, i.e., Judaism, Christianity and Islam, when seen through the lens of logic, will appear to be cases of deductive logic. In this branch of reasoning, the premises are given; such as, Jesus Christ is the only son of God and the Bible lays out what Christianity favours as well as disfavours. Ideally, thereafter, the duty of the faithful is to do what the Bible and the priests in the Church tell. There is very little uncertainty left because of these sources of guidance. The life of the follower in the area of spirituality is simple and smooth. It is like sailing on the unending calm waters of the calmest of rivers.

Unlike Jesus Christ, Allah the Merciful has not visited the earth. Only his blindly trusted Prophet Muhammad lived in Hejaz, the region centred around Mecca and Medina in Saudi Arabia between the years 632 and 642 AD. In the course of these years Allah delivered his whole message or *paigam* through Angel Gabriel when Muhammad saw visions. Subsequently, the message was comprehensively recorded in the *Quran* which is the supreme scripture of Islam. It is the permanent, unchanging compendium for a Muslim to refer to when in any doubt whether spiritual, temporal or personal. Elucidations of the tenets of Islam are laid out in the *Hadith* or the Traditions and *Sunnah* or the life of the Prophet. The Imams, especially through their *khutbas* or Friday prayers add the current issues to inform and guide the *momins* (the faithful).

For a Muslim man, Islam is wonderfully simple with every detail of living laid out. His life is also superior to the woman who is 'half a person' and largely meant for his pleasure, serving him and the religion for multiplying the numbers of *momins*, a programme dear to the Prophet as stated in the Hadith. Modernity is not his domain as modernisation may awaken the woman to her equal rights. Nevertheless, thus, far the deductive prescriptions of the religions originally fathered by Prophet Abraham have helped people of the West to live well and be happy. If they have suffered a bane, it has been the habit of war and more fighting.

The other half of the subject of logic is inductive where, unlike the deductive, there is no premise. There is very little given truth and even less dictated wisdom; not even on the issue of who is God. Sanatana Dharma or what we today know as Hinduism has, at most, shown a direction of where to look for truth and wisdom. The message to the faithful is that one looks for them oneself through one's own karma or deeds. Uncannily, it is not dissimilar to the core of science, specifically physics: for every action, there is an equal and opposite reaction. Each karma has a *bhagya* or destiny as its consequence. What is not deciphered yet is the transmigration of the soul from one birth to the next. How the sins and their punishments or how the virtuous deeds and their rewards are passed on to future lives. The Vedic roots of faith are arguably agnostic and not polytheistic; at most, pantheistic. Deities and avatars like Rama and Krishna are all part of mythology, not all of which is imaginary. For example, the historicity of Krishna has been proved while that of Rama is on the way, if not also on the verge, of being proved.

Karma no doubt would come in the way of sharing the punishment equally of the crimes committed by others; for instance, the leader of the community. That engenders a sentiment of each being for himself. Not that every Hindu knows this consciously, but it must unconsciously be part of his being. In contrast, the Abrahamic followers know that they would eventually be sent to heaven or hell depending on how they have performed in society while they lived. This feeling makes united action easier. The convenient interpretation of karma, however, is faulty. Who has ever said that it is not one's duty to unite with one's fellow beings and fight with them to defend their women and children exactly as one would do for one's own?

When Muhammad Ghori was expected to attack Prithviraj Chauhan to avenge his defeat in the first battle of Tarain 1191, Jaichand, the ruler of Kannauj should have come to the aid of the former. But he did not do so due to a past slight. As it happened, Chauhan was defeated, captured and killed in 1192. That proved to be the end of Hindu rule in Delhi. Before long the same invader sacked Kannauj; Raja Jaichand fled eastwards and was drowned while crossing the river Ganga at Patna. Nemesis did not spare Jaichand for shunning helping Chauhan on the presumption that it was not his duty or karma to do so.

Earlier, Prithviraj Chauhan did not go to the aid of Rani Nayika Devi, mother and regent of Mulraj Solanki when she was threatened by the same Ghori. She had no choice but to fight alone and, as it happened, she defeated the invader. The regrettable fact was the lack of unity. No prince of Rajasthan came to the aid of Maharana Pratap against Akbar. He had to fight alone and spend the rest of his life fighting. A contrarian example was that Rana Kumbha of Mewar, who was supported by Rajput clans, did not lose even against the trinity of the sultans of Gujarat, Ajmer and Malwa. Kumbha ruled from 1433 to 1468 AD. It was he who built the victory tower of Chittorgarh.

In times past, the readiness to ward off an invasion as well as the ability to go out of one's borders and conquer other lands was essential. It was difficult to survive as a successful country without such military preparedness. Hindu kingdoms suffered from this handicap, especially after the advent of Islam. India was on continuous trial during the medieval centuries and its civilization paid a heavy price. The centuries of the medieval period could be called the dark ages of India.

With the end of World War II in1945, the entire situation took an about turn. Two atom bombs fell on the cities of Hiroshima and Nagasaki and brought in their train the nuclear age. On the one hand, several countries stockpiled their arsenals with more nuclear weapons; on the other, using these weapons was strategically forbidden, lest they unleashed irrepressible holocausts. Notwithstanding, conventional weapons continued to be manufactured and traded, and armed conflict continued, beginning with the Korean War, followed by the Vietnam War and several others. That makes the current century one of paradoxes.

Peacemakers employing the magic of meditatio
therefore, become indispensable.

With the Hindu reluctance to gather together an
it is an ideal 'no-war' country. Instead, the Hindu much prefers to succeed by self-actualising himself/herself. By fulfilling oneself completely he/she wishes to achieve a winning karma.

Bloodshed, destruction and economic ruin are seldom the only prices of war. Most of them end without serving any purpose. Take World War I, often termed the Great War by the British, fought between the years 1914 and 1918. It consumed the flower of Europe's youth and emptied the treasuries of all the countries that participated in the fighting. Above all, the War liquidated several of Europe's great empires. The Austro-Hungarian Empire with its capitals at Vienna and Budapest was the successor of the Holy Roman Empire, which in turn was sponsored in 800 AD by the Catholic Church based at the Vatican, was split into nearly a dozen countries. The Russian Czar was dethroned and shot dead with his wife and five children by the Bolshevik revolutionaries. The new rulers were communists who formed the Soviet Union consisting of 16 republics or provinces. The third empire to break up was the Ottoman, which had ruled the Middle East from Istanbul since 1453 AD. The present Turkey was all that remained of the colossus. Germany ceased to be a monarchy; the Kaiser was dethroned and exiled. The British and the French empires survived the war but in a considerably weakened form.

In Germany, the Kaiser was succeeded by the Weimar Republic which was more dysfunctional than functional under multi-party coalitions. Eventually in January 1933, it had to yield its rule to the Nazi regime of Adolf Hitler, n precipitated World War II in 1939. At the end r, Europe as well as parts of East Asia, especially prostrate. From its ashes arose an ambitious Soviet nat became a superpower and wanted to compete rtake the USA. The resulting rivalry was the Cold hich should more appropriately be called World vhich ended in 1991 with the breakup of the Soviet ll in all, the history of the 20th century can be failure of statesmanship and the futility of war. great lesson learnt was how nuclear weapons combat and killing unlike most wars fought that it.

iot that the Western countries that are representative Abrahamic ethos have not tried to abolish fighting and killing. Their motivation might not have been the Hindu consideration but the cruel reality of their own young sons being butchered. America's President Woodrow Wilson, an idealist American leader and statesman took the initiative to form the League of Nations, an association of nations wherein they could discuss, debate and resolve their differences instead of resorting to guns and bombs. The League was a predecessor of the United Nations Organization, which has been working since the end of World War II. Unfortunately, neither the League nor the UN has succeeded in preventing wars. However, one big achievement the UN can claim, is that in its pendency another world war has not taken place, although World War III did take place and end in its time. How much credit can we give to the UNO and how much to the mighty nuclear arsenals of the two superpowers, which was termed the "balance of terror", is a question that needs to be answered?

Without denying the Abrahamic countries the credit for there being no world war since 1945, it is obvious that the acquisitive nature of nations has not diminished over the last seventy-five years. Chinese policies have been aggressive in the hope of acquiring wealth, territory and power. The USA, its critics allege, boosts its economy with the help of its military-industrial complex which, among other steps, needs to make and export weapons. Germany and Japan have learnt a great deal from their defeats and trauma of World War II and have ever since been wedded to restraint. In fact, they have shown the world how to enrich oneself by shunning war or warlike activity. In other words, prosperity and well being are sought and achieved not through depriving other countries of their wealth and bringing it home, but by building their own economies with the help of technology and innovation, as well as international marketing.

The Hindu would say that Germany and Japan have performed economic miracles through sheer *purshartha* (efforts). This is in sharp contrast to what the same nations tried during the war—to conquer other countries and bring home their wealth. They failed in their unethical endeavours and instead brought untold destruction upon themselves. Their examples during the war and after the war are a graphic interplay of karma and *bhagya*, as the Hindu would see. The Abrahamics have historically placed their faith in acquisition, regardless of how, from whom and whether with ethical justification. The concept of dharma is not a principle of Western philosophy; religion yes, but dharma no. This is not to claim that the Hindu has always adhered to a *dharmic* path; no, he has not. But whenever he has not, he has paid the penalty. His suffering under the heel of foreign conquest through the medieval centuries was such a punishment. What could have been the Hindu *dushkarma* or sin? As a conjecture, it could have been the oppression of the dalits who were then called untouchables. Or there could have been other misdeeds.

The Abrahamic propensity to unite is a wonderful virtue when it comes to defending one's society or country. But the same virtue to unite in order to commit aggression on a neighbouring nation or any other is not always weighed on a scale or balance. The first consideration is about the chances of success or failure. To the Hindu, the first thought that crosses his mind is whether the proposal is moral or not. Although in the face of temptation, greed may often push morality into the background. But his awareness that he has been unethical is generally palpable. Ask a poor man why is he poor; most often he would reply that his karma in the past must have been bad. He does not blame the inequity or callousness of the society. He is not generally a revolutionary. In spite of the inordinate poverty of the people, communism, despite having passionate leaders with commitment, failed to make any significant headway in Hindu India.

In a consistent vein, Hindu India has seldom thrown up conquering heroes or empire-builders. Mostly, the instinct of the ruling class also has preferred self-actualisation to aggrandisement. The Cholas of Thanjavur and probably the Pandyans of Madurai went to Southeast Asia and spread the message of Shiva and Vishnu. They created temples and frescoes but were certainly not imperial powers in the Western mould. Germany and Japan have replayed a similar role and touched admirable heights of achievement; they followed the path of self-actualisation, albeit after learning bitter lessons from the destruction of World War II. In contrast, Hindus have learnt the message of self-actualisation through their ancient philosophy, but may have forgotten it, from time to time, while negotiating the corridors of time.

9

The Intolerance of Deductive Logic Adherents

Amalekites

Amalek (Hebrew) is a nation described in the Hebrew Bible or Old Testament as enemies of the Israelities.

According to the Bible, Amalek was the son of Eliphaz and his concubine Timna. Timna was a Horite. Amalek is described as the "chief of Amalek" among the "chiefs of the sons of Esau", from which it is surmised that he ruled a clan or territory named after him.

The Amalekite people were considered to be Amalek's descendants through the genealogy of Esau. In the chant of Balaam, Amalek was called the 'first of the nations'. One modern scholar believes this attests to Amalek's high antiquity, while traditional commentator Rashi states: "He came before all of them to make war with Israel". 1st century Roman-Jewish scholar and historian Flavius Josephus refers to Amalek as a 'bastard' in a derogatory sense.

According to the Bible, the Amalekites inhabited the Negev. They appear to have lived a nomadic or seminomadic lifestyle along the fringes of southern Canaan's agricultural zone. This is probably based on the association of this tribal group with the steppe region of ancient Israel and the area of Kadesh (Genesis 14:7).

As a people, the Amalekites were identified as a recurrent enemy of the Israelites. This role appears in several stories:

- In Exodus17:8-16, Amalek makes war against Israel in the wilderness. Joshua is ordered by Moses to lead Israel in battle, and Moses watches from a hillside. When Moses' hand is raised, Israel prevails, but when it is lowered, Israel falters. So he keeps his hand raised through the entire battle, even having assistants hold him up, so that the victory would go to Israel.
- According to 1 Samuel 30:1-2, the Amalekites invaded the Negev and Ziklag in the Judean/ Philistine border area towards the end of the reign of King Saul, burning Ziklag and taking its citizens away into captivity. The future king David led a successful mission against the Amalekites to recover "all that the Amalekites had carried away".
- In 2 Samuel 1:5-10, an Amalekite tells David that he found Saul leaning on his spear after the Battle of Gilboa and killed him and removed his crown. The intention behind the removal of the crown was for the Amalekite to present it to David, presumably to earn some kind of reward from him. David, however, condemns the Amalekite for killing the anointed king, using his own testimony as reference, and orders his men to execute him.

In Judaism, the Amalekites came to represent the archetypal enemy of the Jews. In Jewish folklore the Amalekites are considered to be the symbol of evil. Nur

Masalha, Elliot Horowitz and Josef Stern suggest that Amalekites have come to represent an "eternally irreconcilable enemy" that wants to murder Jews, and that Jews in post-Biblical times sometimes associate contemporary enemies with Haman or Amalekites, and that some Jews even today believe that pre-emptive violence is acceptable against such enemies. Groups identified with Amalekites include the Romans, Nazis, Stalinists, and bellicose Iranian leaders such as Mahmoud Ahmadinejad.

According to the Midrash, the Amalekites were sorcerers who could transform themselves to resemble animals, in order to avoid capture. Thus, in 1 Samuel 15:3, it was considered necessary to destroy the livestock in order to destroy Amalek.

In Orthodox Judaism, three of the 613 *mitzvot* (commandments) involve Amalek: "To remember what the Amalekites did to the Israelites, not to forget what the Amalekites did to Israelites, and to destroy the Amalekites utterly. The rabbis derived these from Deuteronomy 25:17–18, Exodus 17:14 and 1 Samuel 15:3. Rashi explains the third commandment:

> "From man unto woman, from infant unto suckling, from ox unto sheep, so that the name of Amalek not be mentioned even with reference to an animal by saying 'This animal belonged to Amalek'".

Israelites destroyed Amorites

Deu. 2:33-34: "And the Lord our God delivered him over to us; and we defeated him with his sons and all his people. So we captured all his cities at that time, and utterly destroyed the men, women and children of every city. We left no survivor".

This verse supposedly deals with the wickedness of the Amorite king Sihon of Hesbon, a city of the Amorites (Num. 21:25). They were a wicked people (Genesis 15:16; 2 Kings 21:11). When the Israelites wanted to pass through their land during their exodus from Egypt, the Amorites refused them safe passage and attacked the Israelites. However, they were soundly defeated by Israel (Num.21: 21-31). It is in this context that God delivered them over to the Israelites, that is, in the context of the battle.

Why would the decision of the Amorites be so serious to God that He would have all their people wiped out? The answer is simple. God tells the Israelites why the people were destroyed. It was because of the wickedness of the Amorite people.

Deu. 9.5:"It is not for your righteousness or for the uprightness of your heart that you are going to possess their land, but it is because of the wickedness of these nations that the Lord your God is driving them out before you, in order to confirm the oath which the Lord swore to your fathers, to Abraham, Isaac and Jacob".

God declared that the Amorite people deserved to die because of their sins. They remained unrepentant (unlike Nineveh), and the righteous wrath of God fell upon them via the Israelites. Since all were sinners, all deserves to die. There were no exceptions. Nevertheless, God was merciful by allowing them to live. In the case of the Amorites, God was gracious to them by letting them live and enjoy life with its generic blessings from God (provision of rain, sun, water, etc.,) while He encouraged them to repent of their sins. They refused to turn from their immorality and were finally wiped out.

Also, the death of a child might be a very merciful thing because had the child grown up in the sin of the Amorite culture, it would surely have suffered the eternal wrath of God. If the "age of accountability" notion is correct, then God delivered them into His hands; and it is possible that by this they were spared eternal damnation.

The final and most important reason for their destruction is that God needed to keep the messianic line pure so that Jesus could be born and thereby redeem His people so that believers could go to heaven. Without Jesus' sacrifice, all would be damned. If the Amorites were allowed to live, surely they would have influenced the Jewish nation in a harmful way thereby threatening the arrival of the Messiah. Therefore, God in His righteous judgement executed judgement upon them.

Canaanites wiped out by Israelites

It is a command that led the leading atheist Richard Dawkins to claim that the God of the Old Testament was "a vindictive, bloodthirsty ethnic cleanser ... a genocidal ... megalomaniacal, sadomasochistic, capriciously malevolent bully".

For God had ordered the Israelites to slaughter the apparently sinful Canaanites, saying: "You shall not leave alive anything that breathes. But you shall utterly destroy them." And, according to a passage in the Old Testament's Book of Joshua, they did just that:

"Thus, Joshua struck all the land, the hill country and the Negev and the lowland and the slopes and all their kings. He left no survivor, but he utterly destroyed all who breathed, just as the Lord, the God of Israel, had commanded. He left nothing undone of all that the Lord had commanded Moses." (Joshua. 10:40, 11:15)

The Edomites

Edom was an ancient kingdom in Transjordan located between Moab to the north-east, the Arabah to the west and the Arabian Desert to the south and east. Most of its former territory is now divided between Israel and Jordan. Edom appears in written sources relating to the late Bronze Age and to the Iron Age in the Levant, such as the Hebrew Bible and Egyptian and Mesopotamian records.

The Edomites first established a kingdom Edom in the southern area of modern-day Jordan and later migrated into the southern parts of the Kingdom of Judah. The Tanakh records mention the Edomites and their defeat by Jewish King Saul of Israel in the late 11th century BC. Forty years later King David and his general Joab defeated the Edomites in the "Valley of Salt" (probably near the Dead Sea). An Edomite prince named Hadad escaped and fled to Egypt, and after David's death returned and tried to start a rebellion, but failed and went to Syria (Aramea). From that time Edom remained a vassal of Israel. David placed over the Edomites Israelite governors or prefects, and this form of government seems to have continued under Solomon. When Israel divided into two kingdoms, Edom became a dependency of the Kingdom of Judah. In the time of Jehoshaphat (914 BC) the Tanakh mentions a king of Edom, who was probably an Israelite appointed by the King of Judah. It also states that the inhabitants of Mount Seir invaded Judea in conjunction with Ammon and Moab, and that the invaders turned against one another and were all destroyed. Edom revolted against Jehoram and elected a king of its own. Amaziah attacked and defeated the Edomites, seizing Selah, but the Israelites never subdued Edom completely.

The Hittites

The Hittites, also spelled Hethites, were a group of people mentioned in the Hebrew Bible. They are mentioned several times as living in or near Canaan since the time of Abraham (estimated to be between 2000 BC and 1500 BC) to the time of Ezra after the return from the Babylonian exile (around 450 BC). Their ancestor Heth is said in Genesis to be a son of Canaan, son of Ham, son of Noah.

In the period between 1800 BC and ending sometime before 1000 BC, the Hittites are mentioned about a dozen times as part of an almost fixed formula that lists the "seven nations greater and mightier than the Hebrews" whose lands were to be eventually conquered and exterminated. Five other "major nations" are mentioned in almost all instances of the formula: Canaanites, Amorites, Hivites,Jebusites, and Perrizites. The Girgashites are mentioned only five times. Abraham's covenant in Genesis 15:18 omits the Hivites but includes the Kadmonites, Kenites, Kenizzites and Rephaim.

Islam is an imitation of Judaism and later Christianity, which gave birth to communism. Many anti-communist scholars have stated that the former Soviet Union was actually a state by Jews, for Jews and of the Jews. Many regime changes across Arab world led to the rise of Baathists who were communists themselves. Some of the biggest despots like Syria's Assad and Iraq's Saddam Husain were Arab communists.

10

Hindudom's Missed Opportunities in History

Unlike Arabia, Persia and the north of Africa, plus some parts of southern and Balkan Europe, which succumbed to Islam's onslaught within eighty years, the saga of Hindu resistance to Islam spans over twelve centuries. It took over 500 years for the Arabs and Turks to lay a foundation for their empire in India.

The primary reason for Muslim successes lies with Hindus themselves. They did not study the scriptures and psychology of the barbarian invaders and naively expected that their ancient standards of *dharmic*, i.e., ethical warfare would be reciprocated by the foreign invaders.

The first Islamic attempt on India was by Caliph Umar, who sent a naval expedition to capture Thane in 636 AD. It was defeated and beaten back. Bharuch in Gujarat and Debal in Sind were attacked. The Hindus not only defeated these naval invasions, but also decimated the Arab navy. Yet, they were content with these successes and did not bother to study the looming danger from the west. Meanwhile, chastened by his defeats in India, Caliph Umar was forced to turn his attention to Bukhara, Tashkent and Samarkand.

Caliph Ali sent a large army against Sind in 660 AD or whereabouts, only to be routed with severe losses. Caliph Muawiyah sent six expeditions under Arab armies to capture Sind, all of which met with severe defeats. In 708 AD, another Arab army under the command of Buidal attacked Sind, to meet with yet another defeat. Despite militarily defeating the hordes of Islamic invaders, the Hindus failed to recognise the growing threat from West Asia.

Finally, Muhammad bin Qasim defeated Raja Dahir and captured Sind in 712 AD, but after his recall, there was a resurgence in Hindu power. In 718, Junaid, the governor of Sind tried to attack Gujarat and Kashmir from where he was beaten back by Pulakesin and Lalitaditya respectively. The Arabs were thus, confined to Sind, but the Hindus strangely did not think of counter-attacking and expelling Islam, although they were militarily in a position to do so.

The Islamic barbarian Mahmud of Ghazni, in the course of one of his seventeen invasions of India, attacked the Chandelas in 1018 AD. But when he saw the size of the Chandela army, he lost his nerve and began fleeing to Ghazni. The Chandelas were in a position to finish him off then and there, but in a show of grossly misplaced Hindu generosity, let this monster escape. Had the Chandelas not shown this generosity, India's history would have been vastly different.

In 1033 AD, the nephew of the by then deceased Mahmud of Ghazni, Salar Masood Ghazni attacked India and reached up to the present-day Uttar Pradesh. Hindu rulers united with Raja Suheldev Pasi, and defeated and slaughtered the Islamic invaders to a man. Not a single soldier of Masood's army escaped, with Ghaznavi's nephew too being slain on the battlefield. This crushing rout of an Islamic army kept India safe from foreign invasion for the next century and half, but Hindus made no effort to eliminate the marauders from the subcontinent. As a result, many Muslim merchants and Sufi preachers quietly settled along the western parts of the subcontinent. Many of them acted as spies for later invaders.

Shahbuddin Ghori attacked Gujarat in 1178 AD. The Solankis of Gujarat appealed to Prithviraj Chauhan to forge a joint front, but the Delhi emperor was dismissive of the idea. Ghori eventually attacked and Gujarat's Hindus, on their own, led ably by their Queen Nayika Devi Solanki, inflicted a crushing defeat on the invading Turk army. The sultan of Ghazni escaped alive only by fleeing the battlefield at Anhilwara.

The same Ghori captured the Bhatinda fort in 1189 AD because of its lax defence. Prithviraj Chauhan, enraged at this besieged Bhatinda and in the ensuing battle in 1191 AD, routed Ghori, forcing him to capitulate. He then committed the ghastly blunder of pardoning Mohammad Ghori. The next year, Ghori treacherously attacked Prithviraj's army at night time, a tactic Hindus had till then not heard of. Not only did Prithviraj Chauhan pay for his blunder with his life, the Hindu empire of Delhi and northern India too was extinguished.

Allauddin Khilji of the Khilji Dynasty was most cruel towards Hindus, but Hindu resistance to Islam during his rule too was unrelenting. According to Muslim chroniclers, at the peak of Khilji's rule, the life of no Muslim was considered safe outside Delhi, and the city's gates would be shut at night to "prevent ambushes by the infidel". When

Khilji died in 1320 AD, the law and order situation in the whole of north India was so bad that any moderate ruler from anywhere with an army of not more than 8,000-10,000 could have walked into Delhi. There were a few capable rulers in south India who could have done the job, but they saw this moment to settle their personal scores rather than throw out Islamic rule.

After Timur of Samarkand's invasion of India in 1398 AD and his genocide of Hindus, the Delhi Sultanate lay in a state of anarchy. Islamic commanders plundered the countryside, but Hindus too retaliated. The city of Jalandhar in Punjab was retaken by Hindus in 1431 AD and all Muslims there made prisoner. A Muslim historian Yahya bin Ahmad wrote that the "ruthless infidels had absolutely no respect for the religion of the Musalman". But Hindus failed to find effective leaders in this phase when the Sultanate in Delhi was tottering.

Maharana Kumbhakarna Singh (1433-1468AD), more popularly known as Rana Kumbha, emerged as a mighty and invincible Hindu monarch. A staunch Hindu, Kumbha defeated the sultans of Gujarat, Malwa and Gwalior individually and jointly. Such was the awe he aroused that not even the Delhi Sultanate dared send an expedition against him. Kumbha not only remained unvanquished throughout his life, but also defeated every Islamic invasion against him. Had all Rajput clans united under his banner, he would have erased Muslim rule from India. Sadly, this did not materialise. It was Kumbha who built the famous Victory Tower at Chittorgarh near Udaipur.

Maharana Sangram Singh, or Rana Sanga (1482-1528 AD) as he was known, was another powerful Rajput king. He ruled a powerful Rajput confederacy. Sanga's might can be gauged by the fact that he gave Delhi's Sultan Ibrahim Lodhi a comprehensive thrashing twice, and also defeated the joint armies of the Gujarat and Malwa sultanates. Yet, despite showing Ibrahim Lodhi who was the boss, Sanga had no qualms about letting the Uzbeg adventurer Babar invade Delhi. The Lodhi Dynasty was extinguished in the First Battle of Panipat in 1526. Babar then clashed with Sanga, but his Mughals were badly routed in the first encounter. Only a Rajput traitor Silhadi's defection to the Mughal camp enabled Babar to defeat Sanga in the second encounter. Many historians estimate that even after this defection, had Babar not possessed canons, Rana Sanga would have ended his story that day. Yet, Sanga made no effort to build any ties with Delhi's Rajputs, many of whom served under the Ibrahim Lodhi. Ironically, one of Ibrahim's nephews Mahmud Lodhi, who hated Babar and sought his destruction, allied with Sanga in his war against Babar and perished. This was yet another Hindu opportunity gone abegging.

In 1336 AD, two Hindu brothers Harihara and Bukka founded what went on to become the great Vijaynagara Empire in the south of India. This liberated a large part of southern India. During the time of Krishnadevaraya (1509-1529 AD), the Vijayanagara Empire stretched from Cuttack in the east to Goa in the west, from Raichur in the north to the Indian Ocean in the south. But Hindus did not make use of this great opportunity to erase Islamic rule. Later, weak successors of Krishnadevaraya and the suicidal policy of recruiting Muslim soldiers in the army led to invasion by the combined armies of the Bahmani sultans, and the empire's downfall after the Battle of Talikota in 1565 AD. Muslim soldiers defected en masse in this battle.

The Bijapur Sultanate's most able commander was Shahji Bhonsale. Upon his shoulders rested the power of the sultanate. He failed to see the opportunity to build his own power base. His son Shivaji was quick to see an opportunity and grab it, and thus created history, not only rescuing Hindu dharma but eventually going on to build a kingdom that one day erased Mughal domination in India. Shivaji proved to be a rare Hindu.

Mughal emperor Aurangzeb (1617-1707) was the ultimate in Islamic zealotry, intolerance and jihad upon the Hindus. But the military architecture of his empire rested on the valour and foresight of his Rajput vassal Mirza Raja Jai Singh of Amer. Jai Singh commanded a pan-Rajput stature and respect. Had he rebelled against Aurangzeb, the story of the Mughals would have been over much earlier. But such was Jai Singh's misplaced sense of loyalty that he even declared Aurangzeb to be an avatar of Lord Vishnu!

Eventually, when the Rajputs did rise against the Mughals from 1650-1660 AD onwards, they first refused to join the Mughals in their war against the Marathas and later aligned with the latter. The result was that the Mughals were not only defeated in the Deccan and central India, but their rule over Rajputana too collapsed, with Awadh also passing first into Maratha and later British suzerainty. The Mughals remained confined to Delhi and Palam, until Bahadur Shah Zafar was dethroned following the failure of the Mutiny in 1857 and packed off to die in exile in Burma. This was the formal end of Muslim rule in India. But had Hindus made use of the many opportunities that came their way, Islamic rule might have ended much earlier.

11

Lala Lajpat Rai's Prognosis of the Hindu-Muslim Problem

One of the legendary triumvirate—Lal-Bal-Pal (Lala Lajpat Rai, Bal Gangadhar Tilak and Bipin Chandra Pal) of India's freedom movement against the British colonial rule, Lala Lajpat Rai was a multi-faceted personality and led a life of ceaseless activity dedicated to a selfless service to the nation.

Born in an educated Aggarwal family of Punjab, he studied in Rewari and later in Lahore, capital of the undivided Punjab. He was drawn into one of the most creative movements of revitalization of 19th century India, Arya Samaj, founded and led by Swami Dayanand Saraswati. Later on, he set up a Dayanand Anglo-Vedic School in Lahore.

Lajpat Rai belonged to that period of our history when people like Aurobindo, Bal Gangadhar Tilak and Bipin Chandra Pal had come to see the basic faults in the "Moderate" politics—what they called "political mendicancy" and the inadequacies of gradual constitutional progress. As venerable RC Mazumdar, the doyen of Indian historians explains,

"The ideals of new nationalism preached by its high priests like Tilak, Aurobindo and Lajpat Rai assumed concrete shape, which may be regarded as the precursor of the Civil Disobedience Movement of Mahatma Gandhi". He realised that "the British people were indifferent to Indian affairs and the British press was not willing to champion Indian aspirations" as some moderates believed.

As early as 1897, he had founded the Hindu Relief Movement to provide help to the famine-stricken people thus, preventing them from falling into the clutches of Christian missionaries.

In the two articles Lalpat Rai wrote for the *Kayastha Samachar* (1901), he called for technical education and industrial self-help. In the wake of the Swadeshi movement (anti-partition of Bengal. 1905-1908), when "the idea of a national education caught the imagination of the whole of India", it was Lajpat Rai and Bal Gangadhar Tilak who "propagated the idea". He went to set up the National College in Lahore, where Bhagat Singh studied. When the agitation against increased irrigation rates and higher land-revenue began in Punjab, it was led by the Indian Patriots Association led by Ajit Singh (uncle of Bhagat Singh) and Lajpat Rai would often address their meetings.

As one contemporary British report pointed out, "The head and centre of the entire movement is Lala Lajpat Rai, a Khatri leader. He is a revolutionary and a political enthusiast who is inspired by the most intense hatred of the British government".

For his growing involvement in the freedom movement, he was given the toughest prison sentences in far away Mandalay (now Myanmar) in 1907 without trial. He also led the protest against the horrendous massacre of Jalianwalla

Bagh. Lajpat Rai also visited the USA and Japan where he kept in touch with the Indian revolutionaries. In England, he also became a member of the British Labour Party. In recognition of his outstanding role in the freedom movement, he was elected President of the Indian National Congress at the Kolkata session (1920).As he took much interest in the condition of the working class people, he was also elected as the President of the All India Trade Union Congress.

Lajpat Rai called for "highest devotion and the greatest sacrifice from us" and "our first want, then, is to raise our patriotism to the level of religion, and to aspire to live or die for it".

Lajpat Rai has been seen as "a champion of moral courage than of physical courage" and was aware of the basic problems of the society. Taking lessons from India's millennium old civilizational problems, and learning the correct message from the politics of communal separatism being voiced since long by the likes of Sir Syed Ahmad and his movement, Khilafatists and the pan-Islamists which were taken forward by the Muslim League camp, Lajpat Rai was one of the few leaders who realised the difficulties of an united anti-colonial struggle. He stressed the need for unity in the Hindu society first to get ready for the struggle against the British. That is why, he was actively associated with the Hindu Mahasabha, which had leaders like Madan Mohan Malaviya, and realised that the larger national interest was being sidetracked.

Lajpat Rai had also clearly set out an agenda for socio-cultural resurgence through Hindi and Nagri script, text-books on India's indigenous cultural heritage (many of which were lying in ruins), propagation of Sanskrit literature, *shuddhi* (purification) movement of those whose ancestors were Hindus earlier, and protested against British government's favouritism to non-Hindus.

Gifted with a perceptive mind, he was a prolific writer and authored several works like *Unhappy India*, *Young India: An Interpretation*, *History of Arya Samaj*, *England's Debt to India* and a series of popular biographies on Mazzini, Garibaldi and Swami Dayananda. As a visionary and man with a mission, he founded the Punjab National Bank, the Lakshmi Insurance Company and the Servants of the Peoples Society at Lahore.

A mass leader, he led from the front. While leading a protest march against the all-White Simon Commission in Lahore, Lajpat Rai was brutally assaulted by the British authorities and was seriously injured. This caused the untimely death of this towering freedom fighter in Lahore on 17 November 1928. It was to avenge this brutality that Bhagat Singh took up arms along with Chandrashekhar Azad and made the ultimate sacrifice.

That Lala Lajpat Rai was a great nationalist leader is beyond doubt. But in post-independence India, Marxist historians under Nehruvian patronage declared Lajpat Rai, first an extremist Hindu Nationalist, and then, a communalist or a liberal communalist, afterwards.

The most glaring examples of misreading Lajpat Rai's role in the freedom struggle come from the much acclaimed textbook of modern Indian history, *India's Struggle for Independence, 1857-1947* (Bipan Chandra, et al.) In the two chapters of the book ("The Rise and Growth of Communalism" and "Communalism–The Liberal Phase"), Bipan Chandra has tried to sell the canard that Lajpat Rai was a liberal or moderate communalist. Chandra believed that communalism is "basically and above all an ideology on which communal politics is based". He laments that many nationalists "fell prey to it or thought within its digits" and "saw themselves as Nationalist Hindus, Nationalist Muslims, Nationalist Sikhs, etc. and not as simple nationalist".

What explains this hatred of Marxist historians like Bipan Chandra and his acolytes with Lala Lajpat Rai? And in fact, not only Lajpat Rai, Aurobindo and even Bal Gangadhar Tilak, others were also termed as 'communal' by the Marxists at some point of time.

In a series of articles titled as *The Hindu-Muslim Problem* (1924), Lala Lajpat Rai in his straightforward and incisive prose analysed the conceptions of Islam. He remarked that, "Unlike Hinduism, Islam is a faith of dogmas and doctrines. Every Muhammadan must believe not only in the existence of God without a second (La Allah Il Allah) but also that Muhammad was His prophet and that the Quran is his final word. He must also believe, according to the orthodox school, that Muhammad was the last of the prophets and whatever he said and did is binding on all his faithful followers".

Rai continued, "There have been expounders of Islam who have tried to raise it to a kind of high occultism, but their efforts have not met with any considerable success, and Islam remains, to all intents and purposes, with the majority of its followers, what it has been all through centuries past".

Lajpat Rai didn't pull his punches while criticising the religious intolerance in the Muslims. He observed that, "Religious intolerance of the severest kind has been a handmaid of chivalry, bravery, zeal, learning, and piety among the Muslims throughout Muslim history. Three out of the four first Khalifas were murdered by their fellow Muslims. The pages of Muslim history are full of similar acts done by religious zealots or political adventurers".

These observations were vindicated by the ongoing politics after the Khilafat movement inspired Lajpat Rai, and others like Madan Mohan Malviya to try and test the ground of Hindu politics. The leaders drifted away from the hypocrisies of the Indian National Congress on the 'Muslim Question' and formed an alliance with Hindu Mahasabha. For Marxists, this is their 'ultimate' sin.

However, while Marxist historians heaped abuse on Lala Lajpat Rai, Sri Aurobindo and Madan Mohan Malaviya, they dared not touch Dr Babasaheb Ambedkar, who also stated similar views on the Islamic question.

Dr Ambedkar pointedly suggested that, "The brotherhood of Islam is not the universal brotherhood of man. It is brotherhood of Muslims for Muslims only. There is a fraternity, but its benefit is confined to those within that corporation. For those who are outside the corporation, there is nothing but contempt and enmity... In other words, Islam can never allow a true Muslim to adopt India as his motherland and regard a Hindu as his kith and kin".

Lala Lajpat Rai deconstructed the very discourse of Hindu communalism and completely transformed it, at least in his discourse, into nationalism. In yet another revealing example, he wrote an article on "The Indian Problem" published serially in *The Tribune* (8-10 January 1924) which reiterated his unswerving faith in the necessity of Hindu-Muslim amity for the making of the nation and gaining independence:

> What then is our conception of nationhood? What do we mean by Hindu-Muslim unity? The expression

> Hindu-Muslim unity is only symbolic. It is not exclusive, but inclusive. When we speak of Hindu-Muslim unity, we do not exclude the other religious communities like the Sikhs, the Christians, the Parsis and the Buddhists, the Jains, from our conception of unity or from our idea of nationhood. The Indian nation, such as it is or such as we intend to build, neither is nor will be exclusively Hindu, Muslim, Sikh or Christian. It will be each and all. That is my Swaraj. That is my goal of nationhood.

At best, Lajpat Rai's formulations manifest in the preceding lines can be termed as liberal nationalism and not liberal communalism.

However, Marxists labelled everyone a 'communalist' who dared to touch the vexed Muslim question. Lajpat Rai has been similarly victimised by the Marxists in their state-sponsored textbooks! The true nationalist leaders need to be retrieved for their true contributions.

On the hostility of Muslims in India towards Hindus, Lajpat Rai stated with candour:

> With 70 millions of Moslems, India is the most important centre of Islamic sentiment. The pan-Islamic element is growing stronger. Among the Moslem population of India a large number of Indian Moslems are alive to the importance of India to the cause of Islam in the world.

> The British rallied to their support the newly born aristocracy of the Punjab—the Sikhs. The Sikhs had been persecuted and oppressed by the Mohammedans. They were not in a mood to look favourably at the chance of Mohammedan supremacy being re-established in India. They had had enough of the "Turk," as they called every Mohammedan, and they threw the whole weight of their

recently gathered virility on the side of the British. They believed that in crushing the Mohammedan power, they were revenging themselves on the slayers of Guru Teg Bahadur, the oppressors of Guru Govind Singh and the murderers of his sons.

For a time the Mohammedan minority was the hope of the British Government in India. The bulk of the educated Mohammedans has opposed the Congress, in order to please the Government and win their gratitude; they also opposed the Swadeshi Movement. In return, they received substantial benefits, in the shape of large grants of money for educational purposes, a larger percentage of posts in government service, a larger number of titles and honours, a separate and larger representation in the councils, and so on. Lord Morley confirmed this policy of preference by making it a special feature of his Reform scheme in 1908. In its inception and for some time thereafter the Nationalist movement in India was thus, a pre-eminently Hindu movement.

The events in Turkey, Tripoli, Egypt and in Persia have affected the Mohammedans deeply and have brought about revulsion of feeling against the British. The Muslims are a virile and proud people. The attitude of Britain towards Turkey has offended their deepest susceptibilities and they have begun to think that the British in India wanted to bribe them into silent acquiescence in what was happening to the Muslim people in the other parts of the globe. For the last four years the Muslim press has been carrying on a strong, vigorous pan-Islamic propaganda. The Mohammedan classes as well as masses are full of veiled and subdued hatred of the British. Sometimes this finds expression on the platform, in the press, and in permanent literature too. In the last Balkan war and during Turkey's conflict with Italy about Tripoli, the Mohammedan mosques rang with loud prayers for the victory of Turkey, and with strong and open denunciation of their Christian enemies.

The Mohammedan moderates are wiser than the Hindu moderates. They use their extreme party as a trump card in their negotiations with the Government more effectively than the Hindus do or have ever done. The Mohammedan extremist receives more substantial support and sympathy from his moderate co-religionist than the Hindu extremist does from the Hindu moderates. The Mohammedan moderate is more outspoken in his criticism of government measures that injuriously affect the Mohammedans; he is less lavish in his praises of the British Raj; he is a more skilful negotiator and a decidedly better and more successful diplomat.

The Hindu-Muslim problem is the problem of India. We have heard and read much of Hindu-Muslim unity. The amount of unity or disunity existing at a particular moment is also always an issue. For the last three years Hindus and Mussalmans have been at daggers drawn with each other to an extent never before known under British rule. All attempts to stem the tide have so far proved ineffectual. All efforts for finding a solution have been fruitless. It cannot be denied that at the moment of writing, the relations between the two communities are strained almost to the breaking point. Communal riots and scuffles are of more frequent occurrence than ever before. Mutual distrust and suspicion has reached the point. Even in Congress circles, in spite of much hugging and cooing, the relations between the leaders of the two communities are not free from distrust and suspicion. Hindu-Muslim unity is always put in the forefront of the Congress programme, but so far the leaders have failed to successfully grapple with the situation and find out a suitable solution.

All hopes were concentrated on Mahatma Gandhi, and that person being in jail, it was expected that his freedom would mean the freedom of the country from Hindu--Muslim quarrels. His leadership was acknowledged by all. There was not the least possible suspicion of his motives. He was the very personification of love, forbearance, trust, and goodness. So it was believed that the "key to the Yeravda jail" was the key to Hindu-Muslim unity. Providence in its own wisdom supplied that key, and the Mahatma was released. It is now more than six months that he has been released.

Lalpat Rai had something to say about Mian Fazl-i-Husain and Swami Shraddhanand.

But with all this the document is rather disappointing, and the solution suggested is on the face of it superficial, though noble and magnanimous in appearance. The events of the last six months are enough evidence of its utter failure both as a palliative or and as a curative remedy.

After the above was written on board the ship during my voyage to India, I have had further corroboration of statements made in what I have seen, read, and observed since my landing at Mumbai on the 18th of October 1924. The two shocking [pieces of] news which I heard immediately on landing were about the Kohat tragedy and Mahatma Gandhi's fast. The most disconcerting feature of the former was the total emigration of the Hindus from Kohat, out of fear of further Muslim attacks.

The spectacle of a whole community of about 3,500 men, women, and children marching away from their homes to distant places under Government transport arrangements and with Government help, for fear of being annihilated by an infuriated majority, is, however, a conclusive proof of the falsity of this belief, because it can only mean one of the two things—either the insincerity or the inefficiency of British officials, at least in the North-West Frontier Province. Practically what happened at Kohat was that the authorities considered themselves overpowered and incapable of granting the necessary security to the Hindus. We have often heard of lynch law. What is lynch law? It is nothing else but the prevention of the ordinary course of justice and the preventing of the authorities from proceeding according to law. Was not the happening at Kohat an illustration of the same tendency?

As regards Mahatma Gandhi's fast, it is an open secret that the desecration of Hindu temples, one after another, at Amethi, Gulbarga, Kohat, and, other places, and the tragedy of Kohat, gave him such a shock that he considered it his duty to undergo a penance for his misunderstanding and mishandling the Hindu-Muslim situation during the last three years. For the first time he felt miserable at the thought that he, who had striven his best to obtain Hindu co-operation for the saving of the Muhmmadan "temple" Khilafat, had to see desecration of Hindu temples by tens, in most cases without any provocation, at the hands of Muhammadans.

If the existing conditions are properly analysed it will be seen that sectarianism and narrow-minded bigotry have been very much strengthened within the last three years. The Khilafat movement has particularly strengthened it among the Muhammadans, and it has not been without its influence and reaction on the Hindus and Sikhs.

The non-co-operation movement itself has materially contributed to the creation of this atmosphere. It was unfortunate that the Khilafat movement in India should have taken its stand on a religious rather than political basis. There were political grounds to support it. It was still more unfortunate that Mahatma Gandhi and the leaders of the Khilafat movement should have brought religion into such prominence in connection with a movement which was really and fundamentally more political than religious.

The desire to seek religious sanction for the various items of the Non-Co-operation programme was another great blunder. It led directly to the revival of a sectarian zeal, and to the re-enthroning of influences and forces which were antagonistic to the idea of a united India. Non-co-operation, which was based on the idea of Hindu-Muslim unity, thus, became one of the forces favouring disunity. Never before did I see educated Hindus, Mussalmans, and Sikhs attacking. I have seen young Muslim gentlemen being vigourously attacked by Maulvis for daring to shave their beards, and all India saw the spectacle of a Muslim President attempting to stop the playing of instrumental music at an annual meeting of the National Congress.

I am stating these facts to illustrate my point. Take, for instance, the playing of music before mosques. In my experience of the last forty years I had never felt that the question was of any importance at all, and yet I had been a constant reader of newspapers, and a faithful observer of events. It is similarly a matter of pain to me to notice that some of the most broad-minded Hindus, who have travelled all over the world, should feel the necessity of observing any sort of untouchability towards Muhammadans. I remember a great Samaj leader once denouncing Congressmen for having sold their religion for the sake of unity; and the selling consisted, in his opinion, in their freely eating and drinking with the Muhammadans.

Yet it is an admitted fact that in spite of a rigid caste system and a rigid code of social morality, Hinduism is the most tolerant of all the great religions of the world. Hinduism does not ridicule or despise other peoples' beliefs or faiths: nay it does not question other peoples' right to follow their own faiths and attain spiritual satisfaction thereby. It lays no exclusive claim to be the only royal road to salvation. It is not out to convert other people and thereby save them from hell or perdition. In fact, it expressly lays down that for different people, in different stages of physical, mental, and spiritual developments, there are different ways of approaching God and obtaining satisfaction and salvation. To its own followers it allows the fullest freedom to believe what they like and to worship as they please.

Unlike Hinduism, Islam is a faith of dogmas and doctrines. Every Muhammadan must believe not only in the existence of God without a second (*La Allah Il Allah*) but also that Muhammad was His prophet, and that the Quran is his final word. My Muslim friends will pardon me if I venture to say that too great an insistence on dogma has been the bane of Islam, the cause of its political downfall, and that unless it is given up, it will stand in the way of Islam ever regaining its lost position as a world-wide political factor.

I am firmly convinced that we cannot create a united India and cannot win Swaraj in any shape, unless the religious canker is removed. "*Mazhab*" (in its narrow sense), as my beloved friend Stokes often reminds me, is the curse of India, and as long as it rules supreme, there is no hope for India. The idea that we can remain "good Hindus" and "good Mussalmans" in the narrowest sense of these terms, and yet win Swaraj, is in my judgement, an absurd one. It has done a lot of mischief within the last four years. I still believe that we do not need to depart in any manner or degree from the true and essential spirit of Islam and Hinduism in order to be free and united. There are good and true Christians, Roman Catholics and Protestants, Presbyterians and Anglicans, Jews and Gentiles, in Great Britain, France, and Germany, but the earnestness of their religious faith does not prevent their being free citizens of their respective countries. A hundred years ago, who could have imagined that a Jew would one day be the Prime Minister of Great Britain, another a Secretary of State, and a third a Viceroy of India?

12

Awake and Unite!

After nearly a millennium, a unique opportunity has come our way. The current century can be the Indian century, provided we Indians amalgamate to create a national synergy so that, the efforts of a few Indians lead to the output of many. That is the only way we can generate surpluses in order to leapfrog across lost centuries.

For the greater part of history, brawn has dominated brain, muscle has overruled mind. World War II is an epic example of the resulting brutality. Now, at last, a time has come when the brain is beginning to rule the body. The greed of nations no longer covets the territory of other countries. Colonialism ended decades ago as land ceased to be the principal source of wealth. In the process, trade has replaced war as the instrument for countries to enrich themselves. Indians generally, and the Hindus in particular have preferred trade to war.

At the dawn of this new millennium, there were high hopes and many expectations. With the advent of the computer revolution, we are set to play a big role in information technology. Five million or more Indians are likely to get rich as a result. That is a matter not only of hope but also honour. But India is a nation of a hundred and thirty-eight crores. What about the rest of our people? Just as a chain is as weak as its weakest link, a society is as woeful as its poorest section. Unless we enable all our people to avail of opportunities to be well off, India will not be united enough to seize the opportunity.

Apart from the difference between the poor and the rich, there are several obstacles in the path of Indian unity. The Muslim contempt and hostility, and the Hindu hatred must be overcome. This is the deepest and the widest schism in our society. Without removing or bridging it, India cannot be truly one nation. Many leaders ranging from Emperor Akbar to Sant Kabir and Mahatma Gandhi much later have all failed to bridge this schism, except temporarily or in a few sectors. Their approach was based on placation, whereas mine is on openness and frankness. Unless everyone is empowered to express themselves freely, no true dialogue or understanding can come about. After all, there can be no true friendship without frankness. How can there be a true friendship unless the two speak up the truth about each other?

Women must get their equal place in society. Casteism must go. There should be no need for anyone to feel like a Dalit or a neglected tribal. This book shows how these gulfs can be bridged. Unless every region of the country makes equal progress, national unity will be difficult to sustain. Backward regions would have a grievance while the prosperous areas would consider the poor an economic drag. The vast difference in the employment prospects of those educated in English and the rest has to be removed, if ours is to be a united society.

A bane of our country are the anti-Hindu Hindus who enjoy all the legitimacy of their Hindu pedigree, including names such as Sitaram or Harkishan, and yet spend all their lives trying to divide our society by inciting the poor without reducing their poverty; instigating the Muslim without redressing his grievance. In fact, they form a perennial fifth column. They are a symptom of a masochistic trait or they can be termed as a cancer that destroys the pride and self-confidence of Indians as a nation. How else can India tolerate streets in the middle of its capital New Delhi that commemorate medieval Islamic invaders and iconoclasts?

Suraaj, or a good polity, has to be the ideal that both the Indian state and people should aspire for and work towards. At the core of *suraaj* would be the rule of dharma which requires the leaders to be more ethical than the others. In contrast, under the rule of law, all have equal obligations.

Mahatma Gandhi used to call this *Ram Raj*. To quote his words, "By Ram Raj, I do not mean Hindu Raj. I mean Divine Raj, the Kingdom of God. For me, Ram and Rahim are the same deity". There are many who would baulk at the idea of *suraaj* or *Ram Raj* or *Rajya*, as this carries connotations of a Hindu theocratic state. To answer such misconceptions, one has to be more direct and state that *suraaj* is not in any way visualised as a Hindu state or a theocratic polity. The concept merely represents an ideal state.

Nevertheless, if one were a Muslim cleric, one's mind would flash to the idea of *Dar-ul-Islam*, or what is also often described as *Nizam-e-Mustafa* (the system of the Prophet), an ideal that was born with Islam and has lived with most devout Muslims. Similarly, many a socialist intellectual looks upon the call of *Ram Rajya* as a bugle of revivalism. This would be a case of reading a Hindu ideal with a Marxist mind. If readers were to agree with what I have stated, my request would be for them not to read a Hindu ideal with either a Marxist or Muslim mind. The other fear of many well-intentioned people is that *Ram Rajya* means reviving a state that last existed several thousand years ago since when life has become unrecognisably different.

Here one may submit how a Hindu with a modern mind would view the *Ram Rajya* of the future. The expression *Ram Rajya* denotes an ideal state to Hindus or rather most Indians. Rama personifies *dharma*, whereas a *rajya* means the state whose essential function is to enable each citizen to perform his or her dharma without hindrance by other people. Every citizen would be assured of justice. Dharma is the trinity of faith, duty and morality.

It is essential to iterate here that there is nothing particularly Hindu about dharma. After all, which civilised human being would deny that he has a faith to keep and a duty to perform? Or, shall we say, an *imaan* to cherish and a *farz* towards others. Each citizen has the right to follow his *dharma*. At the same time, he/she has the obligation to allow every other citizen to abide by his dharma. The fundamental function of *Ram Rajya*, as I see it, is to ensure that every citizen has the freedom to fulfil himself, and at the same time not to obstruct any other citizen from fulfilling himself. That is justice.

13

Suraaj and the Rule of Dharma

For a citizen to be just to another, he should be prepared for some self-denial, if not also sacrifice, from time to time. Rama was the epitome of sacrifice. As a gesture of his duty towards his father, he gave up fourteen years of his life in exile or *vanvaas*. For the sake of his principles, he gave up his wife Sita. The king or queen could not afford to carry any blemish. One may recall that a washerman had cast doubt on her chastity during her custody at Lanka.

The moral of Rama's sacrifice was that the higher placed the person, the greater the demand on his conduct. He should not only behave ideally but also be *seen* to be ideal so as to ensure credibility, without which a king or leader cannot command implicit respect. Without such respect, no state can aspire to be perfect. There is nothing religious, communal or Hindu about this.

The essence of *Ram Rajya* would be the rule of *dharma*. The higher a citizen is placed, the greater is the demand on his probity. For example, for anyone it should be sufficient to be honest, but for a minister it might be essential to be seen and known to be honest. If any reasonable doubt is cast even on the integrity of his associates, however near or dear, he must distance himself from those persons, as indeed Rama did from his beloved Sita. Yet, as a tribute to his faith in her fidelity, he did not marry again, nor allowed any other woman to occupy a place in his life.

The conscientious soul that he was, Rama must have experienced exceptional agony. But the duty of kingship superseded the love of a husband for his wife. Ram has been criticised as being unfair not only to Sita but also to his mother Kausalya who was so devastated at Rama's exile that she wanted to accompany him to the forests. But he turned down her wish to share his travails and left her behind at Ayodhya. If he were only a husband or a son, the criticism would be justified.

But the call of the king and country is greater than the duty to mother and wife. This, in fact, is the core difference between the rule of *dharma* and the rule of law which the Anglo-Saxon world of the British and the Americans are so proud of. The rule of law insists on everyone, high or humble, being equal before the law; whereas dharma differs from person to person, for king and commoner.

Justice should be progressive and not equal because people are not equal. The karma of each soul is different; so is his or her *bhagya* or *taqdeer* (fate). If the deeds are different so must be the destiny. Each individual has the liberty to excel in his karma, there being no limits or ceiling on good deeds. At the same time, no one's endeavour to excel should be allowed to curb the efforts of others. Nor should an evil doer be permitted to disturb the karma of the other citizens. The more powerfully placed a person, the greater is his ability to hinder others. Progressive justice must, therefore, be demanding on the powerful, the well placed wrong doer and, at the same time, protective of the commoner.

Another outstanding feature of *suraaj* would be a clean public life, as clean as is humanly possible. If the rule of *dharma* expects those in positions of power to be not only upright but also to be seen to be upright, the least that mere ordinary citizens could do is not to be corrupt. A major cause of corruption is the assumption of excessive functions by the state. More the functions a state assumes, more shall be the number of officers, not all of whom might be above temptation. Lord Acton, English Historian, politician and writer, had said that "power tends to corrupt and absolute power corrupts absolutely". *Suraaj* would therefore find an answer in providing a minimal government to the people.

In any case, the Hindu ethos is based on the liberty of the individual to perform his *karma* to the best of his ability. A welfare state or a socialist state are Western concepts emanating from the Christian belief that God made all men equal but society renders them unequal. The endeavour of a Christian's conscience, therefore, is to try and reform society and to make men equal. If you cannot make a person rich, at least try and teach his children free or cure his sickness. Charity is an endeavour in that direction.

Liberty has to be curbed for the sake of trying to achieve equality. To that extent, liberty and equality stand at opposite ends of the scale. For Indians, *suraaj* would be a state inspired by liberty, which means not only a democracy with complete freedom of expression but also a government which does not breathe down the necks of its citizens. Nor does it do business or run industry, all of which could offer temptation.

Liberty should not be confused with licence for citizens to do what they like. There is a clear dividing line between liberty and licence. The former is the freedom for every citizen to perform his *karma*. The latter is to tolerate a wayward citizen stepping on the toes of fellow citizens and obstructing them. There should be no licence. Minimal government provided by *suraaj* would be strict so that no one is permitted to disturb the liberty of others to do their karmic best. A number of states were categorised by Gunnar Myrdal, the famous Swedish economist and author of *Asian Drama*, as "soft". What he meant was that such a state had a weak government, which is either run by corrupt leaders or which at least could not control corruption. Nor could it ensure the enforcement of law or order. *Suraaj* should be the opposite of a soft state.

The other bane of Indian society that must be done away with is casteism, which is a curse. Untouchability, which is its hideous offspring, is a collective crime.

The practice of untouchability must have driven innumerable persons to crime merely to feed themselves and their children. If avenues of work and employment are barred for any citizen, he might be driven to *dushkarma*—in this regard, against his own better judgement. Let us, however, not forget that untouchability is a collective crime and consequential *dushkarma* resulting in collective *durbhagya*.

In fact, one scar that the social face of *suraaj* must not have is casteism, which is the worst curse of our society. I believe that ill-treatment of the lower castes, especially the Dalits, has been a significant cause of India's ill fate for centuries. To reiterate, untouchability particularly was unforgivable. One might ask what the practice of untouchability or ill-treatment of others has to do with the fate of all of India? As an explanation, let us begin with the assumption that if one is a Hindu one believes that the quality of one's *karma* or deed determines the character of one's *bhagya* or destiny.

Even if one isn't a Hindu, he would understand that many an Indian believes in this cause and effect relation of the Hindu explanation of life. Few know that there are Catholics, especially in Goa, who claim to have been Brahmins. The Bohras of Gujarat are openly proud of their Brahmin ancestry; now they are Shia Muslims. I have met Muslims who insist they were Rajputs and not inferior. The fact is that even conversion to Christianity or Islam has not succeeded in wiping out the memory of caste. It then stands to reason that most would empathise with, if not accept, the Hindu ethos wholeheartedly.

If there is individual *karma*, there must be also collective *karma* resulting in collective *bhagya*. Untouchability was practised not by individual volition but by collective prejudice. It would therefore, be a group crime in which case the whole group has to suffer. This is what I mean when I say that our civilisation has suffered a destiny of invasions, humiliation and exploitation, whether via the Khyber pass or the Indian Ocean. I hope this suffices in highlighting the enormity of the crime perpetrated by the Hindu society. It is true that Mahatma Gandhi and Dr Babasaheb Ambedkar in their different ways did try hard to abolish untouchability. The question is: has all the prejudice disappeared? Even supposing it has to a significant extent, have the disadvantages inherited by the unfortunate generations been wiped out? The answer, evidently, is in the negative.

What is the way out? What is the solution? The reservation of seats in educational institutions and employment positions is helpful but only up to a point. It relieves, one might say, the pain of past prejudice but does it cure the suffering? It is necessary to not only help recover but also to create self-confidence. To keep feeling deprived, to live in the remorse of having been sinned against could lead to self-pity. This, in turn, is an enemy of self-confidence. Nevertheless, there is no dividing line to indicate where help should end and where self-confidence should begin.

A way out of this syndrome should be that each person seeking advantage of a reservation under a caste quota should swear an affidavit that he or she has suffered from the consequences of backwardness and needs the shelter of reservations. Such a procedure should induce many an enterprising youth to not sign the affidavit and be treated as any other citizen of India. In turn, the weaker or a more disadvantaged backward would get an opportunity. This is a process that should help an upward mobility or a move towards social equality.

This is one example of a schematic approach to pull people upwards. It is true that many upper caste Hindus have tried to forget their castes and avoid mentioning their surnames but has that really helped? The collective memory is so deep. After all, castes are as old as Hindu society itself. They began as a method of accommodating a new group of people into the community without it having to lose its individual identity. In other words, castes, to begin with, were not discriminatory but the distinctions eventually turned into an evil as we know it in recent times. Wishing away the evil will not help. The problem has to be faced boldly.

One way of diluting a caste identity is to attract people to a larger loyalty. In this regard, Hindutva or cultural nationalism can play a yeoman role. The prouder we can be of being Indian, the less we will hark back to what else we are. And this includes not merely Hindus but also members of other communities like Christians and Muslims.

Urbanization is a useful antidote to casteism. When a person arrives in a city, he might or might not leave behind his caste prejudices but certainly has to give up many of its practices. Moreover, his children grow up without the prejudices; if the person happens to go in for an inter-caste marriage, so much the better. In Europe and America, up to 95 per cent of the people are occupied in non-agricultural pursuits. Only five per cent or so directly live off farming. In the event, even villages look like small towns and are not a picture of the rural areas with which we are familiar with in our country. It is inevitable that India will also become more and more urban and less and less rural. Today, about 50 per cent of our people in India are directly dependent on agriculture, in contrast to only about five per cent in Europe and America. To that extent, the tide is against casteism.

Apart from societal measures like eschewing caste prejudices, the Indian polity also needs fundamental change. The Constitution of India, which is the world's longest written constitution, is a comprehensive document that empowers the Indian state to be present in just about every facet of the lives of its people. Instead, it should provide for minimal government in order to suit the Indian ethos which is inspired by liberty as distinct from equality.

An example would serve to illustrate this argument. Old-timers might recall that Kolkata was once a centre of hosiery manufacture. I knew of a successful manufacturer who made all kinds of sweat absorbing underwear. He also started making socks as more and more people took to wearing full, as distinct from half, shoes in Kolkata. While *dhoti* was the popular apparel, shoes were worn only by the executive class. In the days of the Raj, the British brought their socks from home. As trousers began to replace the *dhoti*, shoes came into vogue. As years went by, it was suggested to the manufacturer that hosiery gloves would also be fashionable. As with socks, so with gloves; he made one uniform shape. Soon after the sales began, the goods started coming back. The customer complaint was that both the gloves had been woven for the right hand.

What this businessman did to the gloves, India's first Prime Minister Jawaharlal Nehru did to the Constitution. Both overlooked a similar factor, albeit with the best of intentions. No one in the Constituent Assembly pointed out the oversight just as not a single person in the factory could observe the mistake. Constitution making was a Western tradition and therefore, the document was drafted on the implicit assumptions of the Euro-American psyche. The Christian ethos has been pre-occupied with equality: God made men equal but society makes them unequal. Constitution makers, therefore, have strived to achieve equality. The Christian priority was carried forward by Islam until Marxism hit the climax in the appeal for equality.

On the other hand, the Indian psyche evolved on the assumption that *karma* is the cause and *bhagya* is the effect in the life of every individual. There cannot be a ceiling on *karma* or good deeds. Inevitably, therefore, there cannot be any limit to how much good destiny or good fortune an individual might enjoy. In other words, liberty to do good or bad is the mainspring. Although liberty and equality have been made to sound similar due to both being parts of the French revolutionary battle-cry, they actually stand at opposite ends. If liberty is to get free play, it would be difficult to introduce equality. On the other hand, if equality is the desired direction, there has to be a curb on liberty.

In the first place, therefore, the Indian Constitution is made to fit a Western scheme for an Eastern people. Another mistake was that its foundation or skeleton was designed for administering a colony whereas the new document was meant to galvanise a free people to develop. The Government of India Act of 1935, around which our Constitution is structured, was passed by the British Parliament in order to better administer their Indian colony. At the same time, the Act offered a sop to the agitating Indian leaders that they would have some say in the governance of their country. What must be remembered is that the purpose of an imperial power is to keep peace and to cream off the economic surplus of the colony. The opposite is the idea in developing an economy.

A third drawback is that the document is more a patchwork and less of a well-integrated legal document. To the 1935 Government of India Act were added ideas from Westminster. In fact, even today when we are unable to find our own parliamentary precedents, we refer to what happened in the British Parliament. The Westminster model is an unwritten constitution. For instance, the British Parliament is a legislature from which is formed not only the executive government but also the House of Lords, which is the Supreme Court or the Privy Council. Moreover, Britain is a unitary state and not a federation with so many state governments as in India. How then can a unitary sample be used for cutting a federal coat?

The Constituent Assembly of India imported the model of the American Senate for our upper house. On way to the distant Indian shores, the shape of the Senate got distorted. Every state in the USA, regardless of its size, elects two Senators and that too by universal adult franchise. By the time the concept of US Senate was adopted for the Indian

Constitution the representation to the upper house was proportionate to the population. The very spirit of equality amongst the federating units was jettisoned. Instead of public voting, the electorate of the Indian Senator or Member of Parliament were the members of his own state assembly. The framers of our Constitution also borrowed from other documents like those of Ireland, the then Soviet Union and Switzerland. The act of blending laws, rules and regulations was such as to put a brake on progress. There was little consideration for decision making or implementation.

We borrowed the idea of the Rajya Sabha from the Senate with also the intention of making the vice-president of the country the chairman of the Rajya Sabha. But the President or the Rashtrapati was a kind of a copy of the British constitutional monarch who reigned but did not rule. The Lok Sabha is on the pattern of the British House of Commons whose members are voted as legislators or law makers. Having been elected, they also turn into the bearers of the executive. It is the majority of the legislators that elects the prime minister, who then chooses his ministers or his executive from amongst the men and women elected by the people as legislators. The Indian prime minister has to be continuously vigilant in order to ensure that he does not lose the support of the majority. He, therefore, does not have a free hand but works only at the pleasure of this majority. No wonder that the government moves so slowly.

Four years after the Constitution was adopted, a committee was appointed in April 1954, headed by Nehru himself to study the question of changes in it. By that time, the Constitution had already been amended (the First Amendment was passed in June 1951). In May 1976, the Swaran Singh Committee was appointed to go into the question of amending the Constitution.

In fact, the Haryana, Punjab and UP assemblies went to the extent of passing a resolution asking for the reappointment of a new Constituent Assembly which would write a fresh Constitution. By now, the document has been amended 125 times! On the contrary, in the course of 225 years, the US Constitution has been amended only 26 times. The Japanese Constitution, adopted in 1947, has not been amended even once.

All these facts point to an admission of mistailoring at the first instance. The coat was cut without clearly studying the idiosyncrasies of the wearer, the people of India. We agree that liberty is the mainspring of the Indian ethos. Freedom extends to each individual to seek salvation through a path of his/her own choice, be it *bhaktiyoga* or blind devotion, be it *karmayoga* or the path of rightful action, be it *jnanayoga* or self-realisation, or be it any other path. The individuals are free to achieve *mukti*, *moksha* or the liberation of their soul from having to be reborn.

The implication of this liberty is that an Indian does not necessarily have to perform his *karma* within society. In contrast, a Christian or a Muslim would be judged on Doomsday by God as to how well he/she did by society, whether he or she is fit to go to heaven or deserves to be sent to hell. There is no concept in the Judaic ethos for *sanyas* or *samadhi*. The commitment to social or civic contribution is distinctly greater. The corollary should be a sharp dividing line between public wealth and private interest. Even a dishonest person is aware that he is sinning if he were to take advantage of public wealth. Such a society could afford a government that undertakes many functions, whether welfare, charitable or otherwise. These, in any case, might be necessary to ensure equality amongst the citizens. One has to bear in mind that the Judaic complaint has been that God made men equal but society makes them unequal.

A clean public life must be an outstanding characteristic of *suraaj*. To ensure that, it is necessary to jettison the Westminster model in favour of a structure that would suit the Indian circumstances. In order to give the people of India an opportunity to get used to the new structure, the beginning could be confined to the States. In due course, thereafter, the experience should be transferred to the Centre. All executive powers should be given to a trinity of governors. In a universal adult franchise election, the first three candidates should become governor, vice-governor and deputy governor respectively. Within the troika, each of them should have a voting right proportionate to the votes he or she secured in the public election.

The term of office of the troika should be six years. But none of them would be eligible for re-election to any public office within the state. This provision should help to ensure that the three men or women would concentrate on good governance rather than doing favours in order to get re-elected. The intention behind three governors is to avoid putting all the state's eggs in one basket. Moreover, three would be able to represent a fuller profile of the state's populace than one person. The legislators would then concentrate on making and monitoring laws. Except that a two thirds majority of the assembly passing a vote of no-confidence against any of the governors would be a serious step. Their lack of confidence should be referred to the Rajya Sabha, the majority of whose members would have the final say on the assembly's verdict.

The long and short of this argument is that the Constitution for India should provide minimal, rather than comprehensive government. The less patronage the government has, the greater are the chances of a clean public life. The government should be minimal enough to give the people plenty of freedom and opportunity. It must strictly ensure that this liberty does not allow one citizen to step on the toes of another and thus, interfere with his freedom to act. In other words, liberty should not extend to licence and the government must ensure that everyone enjoys equal freedom, whether in the pursuit of his profession, his business, his worship, or any other pursuit of life.

Nationalism should create national synergy whereby the effort of four Indians would result in the output of about five or six.

Some educated and forward-looking Indians do have an instinctive grasp of nationalism as a concept. I wonder whether this grasp has anything to do with modern education, which arrived in India with the advent of the British. I say this because of all the communities and religious groups that have operated on a world scale, it is the Western European Christians who contributed most to the evolution of nationalism and practised it as a political philosophy.

In contrast, most Jews, no matter where they live, candidly show their first sympathy for Israel. Until 1924, there was the *khalifa* (Caliph) who was, at least symbolically, the spiritual as well as the temporal head of all Sunni Islam. The communist is, *per se*, an internationalist owing his first loyalty to the workers of the world rather than to the government of his country, if at all.

As I have mentioned earlier, *suraaj* is our ultimate goal. The question is how to get there. There is no short cut and the only way to achieve the objective is with the help of nationalism. Unless our country becomes nationalist, it is going to be well nigh impossible to become modern, leave alone a *suraaj*. And what is nationalism?

To put it simply, a nation is the extension of a joint family. It is the macro or the enlargement of what is micro or small as represented by a family. Most people usually have a common tradition and a shared memory which is often called a common consciousness. Usually they speak the same language and worship similar gods, but not necessarily so. When someone in the family marries a lady from another part of the country or the world, she may speak a different language and profess a different faith. But she can still be very much an integral part of the family. The ultimate test of her membership is her loyalty to the family.

In exchange for this loyalty and love, the individual experiences a sense of belonging and a sense of security. The family roof offers shelter and protection. The family's goodwill gives the individual an identity, legitimacy and respectability. To belong to a nation, therefore, is to save oneself from the loneliness of an orphan or the diffidence which is often associated with an illegitimate child.

Property, whether land or building, gives the joint family a physical base. It provides a material bond to the members and the promise of a refuge in times of adversity. Territory is similarly the nation's property. Without it, the nation disperses just as the joint family disintegrates when it does not have its land or buildings. The Jewish nation is a classic example. After its diaspora or dispersal from Palestine, over 20 centuries ago, the Jewish people had no territory. The people dispersed to settle as far away as India, Iran, Russia, Germany, Poland and the USA.

The ill treatment of the Jews has a long history. Anti-Semitism is a common expression. Except in India, they were discriminated against everywhere. In Europe, they could neither own land nor obtain state employment. The climax of their tragedy was the extermination of six million Jews by Adolf Hitler before and during World War II. What a colossal price for a people to pay for not possessing territory! This should be a useful reminder to those Indians who do not recognise the sanctity of our Motherland and who object to the prayer "Vande Mataram".

After a long struggle, the Jews were able to acquire a part of Palestine as their territory. In 1948, the State of Israel was established with a small population including those who had been immigrating since 1882. It was indeed an old national dream at last come true. The Jews behaved like a nation possessed. With energy and determination, they have built up a country of Jews who inspire awe in the hearts of millions of Arabs across West Asia! Such is the magic of a motherland.

What is the practical value of nationalism? The answer is simple. No society has successfully graduated from the medieval, agrarian stage of history to the modern industrial era without the energy of nationalism. The communist countries were those exceptions that tried to take a historic leap into the modern age without the help of a nationalist spirit. In fact, they deprecated nationalism and claimed they were internationalist. Their call was for the workers of the world to unite.

The Soviet Union led this experiment which, as the world knows, ended in disaster. The failure was similar in its Eastern European satellite countries. Be it Poland, Hungary, Czechoslovakia or Romania, all have abandoned communism. The contrast between North and South Korea is also telling. Nationalism shouldn't be confused with either liberalisation or democracy. South Korea's regime was autocratic until quite recently. The Chinese leadership after Mao Tse Tung was wise enough to see reality and abandon its internationalist posture. Today China is a picture of Han (their race) nationalism.

Contrast the Russian disaster with the Japanese miracle. An island country with few natural resources;—see how it is aspiring to become the wealthiest nation on earth. It is all the more astounding when one recalls the devastation Japan suffered in World War II. The atomic bombing of Hiroshima and Nagasaki in 1945 is still green in world memory. As a people, the Japanese are extraordinarily single minded in their purpose; to the extent of being obsessed by their objective. But that alone would not have taken them so far. What has made the overwhelming difference is their nationalism carried, as it were, to perfection in unity.

The whole nation has one supreme goal: to improve technology, make better and better products and to export more and more of them. What is unique is how the whole nation puts its collective shoulder to the wheel of this supreme goal. Every Japanese man, woman and child, whether he/she is in industry, farming, government or municipality, is preoccupied with the supreme goal. This explains the nature of their exceptional achievement.

Contrast the Indian stagnation with the Japanese miracle. In 1945, India was better placed than the war ravaged Land of the Rising Sun. Yet our country kept fumbling: going forward in some areas, receding backwards in others and marking time in many others. If there be one reason for this stagnation, it is the neglect of nationalism for all the decades since Independence.

The collective memory or consciousness of virtually all Indians is about the same. Whether it is described as Hindu, Bharatiya or Indian, it amounts to the same. The ancestors of most Indians were at some stage or another Hindu. A community like the Parsis came from Iran and have maintained their separate identity. But over the thousand years that they have been here, they have imbibed more than enough of the Indian ethos to be, politically speaking, one with the rest. The position of the Jews may be comparable.

True, a small percentage of the Muslims who came to India may or may not share the same consciousness. But even two or three centuries are not a short time. And who can claim to be of pure foreign blood? In any case, many of those who had strong non-Indian leanings migrated to Pakistan. There was no Islam even in most of what is now Pakistan until the 13th century. Even Sind and Baluchistan had none till after the coming of Mohammed bin Qasim in the 8th century.

The essence of cultural nationalism was captured by Sir Syed Ahmad Khan, the founder of the Aligarh Muslim University in a speech he delivered in 1884 "*British Paramountcy and Indian Renaissance*" (*Eminent Mussalmans*, Natesan) "Do you not inhabit the same land? Remember that the words Hindu and Mahomedan are only meant for religious distinction—otherwise all persons, whether Hindu or Mahomedan, and even Christians who reside in this country, are all in this particular respect belonging to one and the same nation". In another speech he referred to the Hindus and Muslims as forming one nation. To a Punjabi Hindu audience he said that every inhabitant of Hindustan is a Hindu, and added "I am therefore, very sorry that you do not regard me as a Hindu" (*India Divided*; by Rajendra Prasad).

The seed of Hindutva was sown some 3,400 years ago by Shri Krishna who dreamt of a pan India and who sent his message as for as the present day Waziristan in the north, Manipur in the east and Tamil Nadu in the south.

It is true that the expression 'cultural nationalism' is regarded to have been first used by Rajnarain Bose, the grandfather of Sri Aurobindo, way back in the 19th century. This, however, should not lead anyone to believe that Hindutva is as recent as that. Nor was it a reaction against either Islamic or Christian pressure. The basic inspiration was that the whole of India, despite all its diversity, was essentially one. The significance of the word 'cultural' is also to distinguish this nationalism from a religious impulse. Even today, the central thrust of Hindutva is national unity.

The concept of nationalism, as distinct from mere unity, is comparatively new. Its seed was sown by the Reformation which overtook Christianity in 16th century Europe. The plant, however, blossomed some two centuries later with the rise of the mercantile class, as distinct from the landed aristocracy, quite a part of which was the clergy that controlled the churches of Europe. The inspirational base of nationalism became useful in reducing the power of monarchy. In fact, until the advent of nationalism, there was little by way of a political ideology except as provided by religion or rather Christianity.

Nevertheless, the desire of the Indian civilization to underline its unity was first demonstrated as long ago as some 3,400 years. It was Shri Krishna who first personified the unity of India. On his shifting from Mathura to Dwaraka, Sri Krishna went on to become president of the

Andhaka-Vrishni league or confederation of five Yadava republican committees. They were situated on the west coast of what is now called Saurashtra, the great peninsula in Gujarat. The area was called Prabhas and the capital was at Dwarakapuri.

The city of PrabhasPatan still throbs with life and activity. It is only a few kilometres from Somnath. The constituent members of the Andhaka- Vrishni league had their differences and could not pull together. Shri Krishna was keen to ensure unity but his efforts eventually came to naught (*The Republican Trends in Ancient India*, by Shobha Mukherji 1969).

He realised he was ahead of his time and yet, being wedded to the idea of political unity, Shri Krishna charted a new path. He guided and supported the Pandavas in the epic war. Eventually they emerged victorious and established a united kingdom at Hastinapura. Soon thereafter, Yudhisthira was advised to perform the *ashwamedha* or the horse sacrifice with the political intent of expanding the state. In the words of AD Pusalker (*The History and Culture of the Indian People* BhartiyaVidya Bhavan) there is now a broad agreement about the historicity of Krishna.

Having failed to achieve political oneness with the help of republics forming a confederation, Shri Krishna evidently went on to support King Yudhishthira to consolidate a united kingdom presumably in hope of promoting an expanding unification. The presumption is based on the universal adoration Shri Krishna personally received then and which is perpetuated to this day.

Everyone, at least in India, realises what Shri Krishna means to the Hindu psyche. Just as Shri Rama exemplifies the uncompromising idealist, Sri Krishna personifies the comprehensive realist. When a Hindu has a problem, he wonders what Keshava would have done to solve it with his genius for tactic and strategy. If the Hindu wants to understand what life is about, he resorts to the *Bhagwad Gita*. If he wishes to celebrate a festival he thinks of Giridhar Gopal. If he desires frolic, he sees Gopinath. If he looks for love, he cannot but help dreaming of Radheyshyam. Keshava, Giridhar Gopal, Radheyshyam, Gopinath, Kanha, are some of the many names by which Shri Krishna is called, referring specifically to different facets of his personality.

No doubt, Shri Krishna is more woven into the soul of Indians than any other *avatar*. The *Bhagwad Gita* is a gem of a philosophy, not a religious commandment, nor even a piece of mythology. Shri Krishna was predominantly a strategist, whether in diplomacy or in war. His soul was evidently wedded to a united India. Or else, how could he still be adored literally from Kashmir to Kanyakumari and from Kamrup to Kutch? Manipuris on the Myanmar border are predominantly devotees of Shri Krishna. It is believed that Arjuna visited this border state whose princess Chitrangada was married to him. Arjuna was also reputed to have conquered a number of other territories. Similarly, his younger brother Nakula went westwards and made quite a few conquests on the banks of river Sindhu as well as Saraswati. Incidentally, the south was also not neglected; the Iyengars of Tamil Nadu are devotees of Shri Krishna. In Tamil, Krishna is called Kanna and Kannan is quite a popular name.

What else is this but cultural nationalism or Hindutva? Having accepted Shri Krishna as the fountainhead or rather the Gangotri of Hindutva, let us move to Vishnugupta Kautilya in the fourth century BC. A great deal of his life and work are mixed between the light of history and the mist of legend. Traditionally the Hindu is more a speaker or a listener; less a reader and a writer. In the event, ancient history is less recorded than could be. Or else we might have discovered more figures who personified Hindutva. However, we focus more hereon recorded history.

Kautilya was the friend, guide and philosopher of Chandragupta Maurya who was the greatest emperor that the subcontinent had known until then. He ascended the throne of Magadha at Pataliputra in 321 BC. In the context of Hindutva, his achievements were several. He defeated and expelled all foreigners, specifically the Greek conquerors and their garrisons from the soil of India. His empire comprised all of north and a large part of eastern India. There was an urge for a pan-Indian oneness. Behind it the brain was Kautilya's and the brawn was the emperor's whose grandson Asoka carried the march forward.

Asoka's empire was larger than his grandfather's but for the purpose of Hindutva we are not concerned with imperial success. The question is who inspired or initiated a new drive towards the oneness of India. Adi Shankaracharya did a great deal more than all the emperors taken together. Although there is a controversy about the century in which the Acharya lived his thirty-two hectic years, circumstantially we take it to be 8th century A.D. (*Adi Sankara—His Life and Times* by TMP Mahadevan). He is believed to have been an *avatar* of Lord Shiva. For the purpose of Hindutva, however, our interest is confined to his consciousness as to the oneness of India. And the fact that he travelled the length and breadth of the subcontinent more than once was no easy task to have been undertaken on foot for someone who was based in Kalady in Kerala. He established the four *dhams*, namely, Dwaraka, Badrinath, Puri and Kanchi/Rameshwaram. The mission of Adi

Shankaracharya went a long way in proving the essential integrity of India. He is an important link in the long chain of Hindutva.

Traumatised by invasions, Hinduism survived with the help of its bhakti saints who took the spirit of the Hindu faith to the masses. Chhatrapati Shivaji waged a struggle for Hindu revival.

During the medieval period, the cause of Hindutva was pursued socio-religiously through a galaxy of *bhakti* saints. They played a yeoman's role in integrating the caste-ridden Hindu society. They helped to transfer the Hindu ethos from the philosophical to the devotional, from the intellectual to the popular, from the meditational to the mystical level. The benefits of the culture were distributed widely from the portal of the learned to the hutment of the commoner.

Ramanuja was the first and the greatest among the Vaishnava mystics. He died in 1137 AD. Madhva was a Kannada Brahmin who founded a sect known by his name in the following century. About the same time, the Telugu Brahmin Nimbarka settled near Mathura to sing the praises of Shri Krishna and his consort Radha.

In Maharashtra, between 1271 and 1296 AD, Jnaneshwara wrote the *Bhavarthadipika*, a commentary on the Bhagwad Gita, which proved to be the fountainhead of devotionalism in this region. Namdev, 1270 to 1350 AD, was a tailor by caste who took to the *bhakti* of Vithoba, an incarnation of Vishnu, at the still popular temple at Pandharpur. He was surrounded by several holy men who had, like him, humble origins; some of the prominent ones were Gora the potter, Samvata the gardener, Chokha the untouchable, Sena the barber and Janabai the maid.

Two centuries later came Eknath who revived the *bhakti* tradition in Maharashtra. He gave the people a popular commentary on the *Ramayana*. Above all, he showed how every Hindu could aspire to the deepest religious experience no matter how many obstacles the Muslims put in his way, for example, by razing temples to the ground as had been done to the one at Pandharpur.

As is well known, Tukaram, 1598 to 1650 AD, was the outstanding *bhakti* poet from Maharashtra. Ramdas, (1608 to 1681 AD) orphaned as a child, left home and, after long years of spiritual training and wandering, settled down on the banks of the river Krishna where he built temples of Sri Ram. The threat of Islam was on his mind. He, therefore, stood for activism and Shivaji, the great Maratha ruler, was his pupil.

In Bengal, devotionalism had several inspirations; the Vaishnava impetus began with Jayadeva and his *Geeta Govinda*. Chandidas, in the 14th century was an unforgettable name in *bhakti* literature. Then came the even more famous and revered Chaitanya who lived, sang, danced and reformed between 1485 and 1533 AD.

The Hindi heartland also produced its galaxy of *bhaktas* or distinguished devotees. Sri Ram was the more popular *avatar* unlike the other areas where Sri Krishna inspired more *bhakti*. Ramananda, 1400 to 1470 AD, was the first of the great *bhaktas* followed by Kabir who was four decades his junior. Tulsidas was the other famous spiritual heir of Ramananda. He wrote the *Ramcharitamanas* which really was the *Ramayana* in Hindi instead of the original Sanskrit by Valmiki. The blind Surdas, who lived earlier between 1483 and 1563 AD, expressed his devotion through song and music.

This mystic outburst across north India led to the growth of the popular languages later called vernaculars by the British to distinguish them from the classical Sanskrit, Pali or Ardhamagadhi. As the epics were translated or rewritten, as for example Tulsidas' *Ramacharitamanas*, literature flourished in prose as well as poetry. Countless *bhajans* or devotional songs fertilised both verse and music.

Sankaradeva in Assamese, Chandidas in Bengali, Vidyapati in Maithili, Narsi Mehta in Gujarati, Mira Bai in Rajasthani, Kabir in Bhojpuri-cum-Urdu, Surdas in Brajbhasha, Namdev and Eknath in Marathi, Saraladas in Oriya and above all Guru Nanak in Punjabi contributed not only to *bhakti* but also to the popular languages and literature.

"Why should we remain content with what the Muslim rulers choose to give us? We are Hindus. This whole country is ours by right, and is yet occupied and held by foreigners. They desecrate our temples, break holy idols, plunder our wealth, convert us forcibly to their religion, carry away our womenfolk and children, slay the cows and inflict a thousand wrongs upon us. We will suffer this treatment no more. We possess strength in our arms. Let us draw the sword in defence of our sacred religion, liberate our country. Are we not as brave and capable as our ancestors of yore? Let us undertake this holy mission and God will surely help us. We are the captains of our fortunes and the makers of our freedom", said Shivaji.

A close look at Shivaji's life discloses his intense regard for religion. He indeed cared more for religious emancipation of his land than mere political dominion. The religious persecution practised by Mohammad Adil Shah and Aurangzeb moved Shivaji intensely and influenced his actions. At the same time he realised that religious freedom could not be obtained without political power, and to that extent, he exerted himself in freeing his homeland from Muslim control. As a result of his visit to the emperor's court he was perhaps convinced of the hollowness of the Mughal Empire, and thereafter exerted himself in bringing India under Hindu control. The imposition of *chauth* or one fourth revenue on lands outside his immediate sway was a means to that end. His coronation ceremony and the grand title he assumed suggest his intention of establishing a Hindu empire, certainly by degrees, according to his means. His expedition to Karnataka was a clear move towards a Hindu India in which pursuit he roped in Qutab Shah of Hyderabad. If he had been gifted with a longer span of life, he might have brought about the deposition of Aurangzeb, so clearly emphasised a little later by his son Sambhaji in his Sanskrit letter to Ram Singh. That Hindustan is essentially a land of the Hindus, and other similar phrases scattered throughout Sanskrit and Marathi literature are sentiments actuated by Shivaji's endeavour, closely followed after him by the Peshwas. Mahadaji Scindia indeed felt the glory of having achieved some of these dreams when he attained supreme power at the court of Delhi. The Peshwas, over several generations, carried the Maratha *bhagwa* or saffron flag far and wide, as did the other Maratha families like the Scindias, the Holkars and the Gaekwads. The territories they captured ranged from Attock (present-day Balochistan) in the north, to Karnataka in the south; from Bengal in the east to Gujarat in the west.

With the advent of the British intervention, the Hindu renaissance began.

The tide of Hindutva in the 19th century AD was inaugurated by Rajnarain Bose and Nabagopal Mitra who, in 1886, started the Hindu Mela. The latter also set up gymnasia that became training schools in martial arts, teaching Bengali young men to wield the *lathi*, the dagger and the sword. The wealthy zamindar Debendranath Tagore, father of Gurudev Rabindranath Tagore, lent his support to the Hindu Mela.

With the publication of the novel *Anand Math* in 1882, Bankim Chandra Chatterji offered the next milestone for those marching on the road of Hindutva. "Vande Mataram" overnight became the anthem of Hindutva. Many a sentence contained in *Anand Math* epitomised the essence of nationalism:

> "He (the child) alone is worthy of this duty who has renounced everything for the sake of Mother India. The man whose heart is tied with the string of human attachment is like a kite that is tied to the reel; it cannot fly high or far from the earth below".
>
> "Splendid! Do you both renounce your castes? For all children belong to the same caste, in our work there is no Hindu or Muslim, Buddhist or Sikh or Parsee. We are all brothers here—all children of the same Mother India".
>
> "I want to tell you that this country belongs to us. This is our motherland. Why don't you Englishmen, like true Christians, return peacefully to your own homeland?"
>
> "I have addressed only my Mother India as mother. I can never allow myself to cause my husband to leave his path of duty. If my husband has to die at your command, let him die. I can never, never ask him not to die".

Swami Vivekananda awoke the interested Western world to the wisdom that is Hinduism. This perennial explanation to the mysteries of life on earth was unknown to almost everyone in Europe and America. He began his international mission in 1893 at the Parliament of Religions held at Chicago. In that event, he laid the foundation of acquiring legitimacy for Hindutva in eyes of foreigners. If only we could today communicate half as well as he did, single handed, in a matter of a few years, Hindutva may well become the world's dominant ideology. To quote a few of his sentences:

> The one common ground that we have is our sacred tradition, our religion in Europe, political ideas form the national unity. In Asia, religious ideals form the national unity. The unity in religion, therefore, is absolutely necessary as the first condition of the future of India. What do I mean by one religion? Not in the sense of one religion as held among the Christians, or the Mohammedans, or the Buddhists. There are certain common grounds; and within their limitations this religion of ours admits of a marvellous variation, an infinite amount of liberty to think and live our own lives.
>
> We see how in Asia, especially in India, race difficulties, linguistic difficulties, social difficulties and national difficulties, all melt away before this unifying power of religion. We know that to the Indian mind there is nothing higher than religion's ideals, that this is the keynote of Indian life ... it is the only possible means of work; work in any other line, without first strengthening this, would be disastrous. Therefore, the first plank in the making of a future India, the first step that is to be hewn out of that rock of ages, is this unification of religion.

> We have seen that our vigour, our strength, nay our national life, is in our religion. You have withstood the shocks of centuries simply because you took great care of it. You sacrificed everything else for it. Your forefathers underwent everything boldly even death itself, but preserved their religion. Temple after temple was broken down by the foreign conqueror, but no sooner had the wave passed than the spire of the temple rose up again. Some of these old temples of southern India and those like Somnath of Gujarat will teach you volumes of wisdom, will give you a keener insight into the history of the race than any amount of books. Mark how these temples bear the mark of a hundred attacks and a hundred regenerations, continually destroyed and continually springing up of the ruins, rejuvenated and strong as ever.

Swami Dayananda's outstanding contribution was the revival of *shuddhi*. This was an ancient Hindu concept of purifying any Hindu, through prescribed rituals, who got polluted. For instance, crossing the ocean of black waters or the seas was often considered a cause of pollution.

The second use of *shuddhi* was for the reinstatement of a lapsed Hindu like someone who, or whose ancestor, had got converted, say, to a religion of the book. During the medieval period or the dark ages of Hindutva, this ancient custom was forgotten. The *Atharva Veda* prescribed the rite *vratyastoma* for readmitting those who had fallen beyond the pale of society.

The Swami was awakened to the need for introduction of *shuddhi* at Kolkata, which he visited in 1872, perhaps as a result of his contact with Brahmo Samaj leaders like Keshub Chandra Sen. For Hindutva, the Swami's was indeed a contribution of great potential. Remember that the overwhelming majority of Christians and Muslims in our country are lapsed Hindus. It is quite possible that some of them someday may wish to return to the Hindu fold. How can anyone be welcomed unless there is a gateway? Dayananda reopened the gate which had been shut and forgotten for centuries.

Shri Aurobindo was another sage whose thinking has enriched the philosophy of Hindutva. In 1907, he wrote:

> Nationalism depends for its success on the awakening and organizing of the whole strength of the nation: it is, therefore, vitally important for nationalism that the politically backward classes should be awakened and brought into the current of political life, the great mass of orthodox Hindustan which was hardly even touched by the old Congress movement, the great slumbering mass of Islam which has remained politically inert throughout the last century, the shopkeepers, the artisan class, the immense body of illiterate and ignorant peasantry, the submerged classes, even the wild tribes and races still outside the pale of Hindu civilisation. Nationalism can afford to neglect and omit none.

> In 1908, he wrote: The new nationalism overleaps every barrier; it calls to the clerk at his counter, the trader in his shop, the peasant at his plough; it summons the Brahmin from his temple and takes the hand of the Chandala in his degradation; it seeks out the student in his college, the schoolboy at his book, it touches the very child in its mother's arms; and the secluded *zenana* has thrilled to its voice; its eyes searches the jungle for the santhal and travels the hills for the wild tribes of the mountains. It cares nothing for age or sex or caste or

> wealth or education or respectability; it mocks at the talk of a stake in the country; it spurns aside the demand for a property qualification or a certificate of literacy. It speaks to the illiterate or the man in the street in such vigorous language as he best understands, to youth and the enthusiast in accents of poetry. In language of fire to the thinker in the terms of philosophy and logic, to the Hindu it repeats the name of Kali, to the Mahomedan it spurs to action for the glory of Islam. It cries to all to come forth, to help in God's work and remake a nation, each with what his creed or his culture, his strength, his manhood or his genius can give to the new nationality. The only qualification it asks for is a body made in the womb of an Indian mother, a heart that can feel for India, a brain that can think and plan for her greatness, a tongue that can adore her name, of hands that can fight in her quarrel. The new Nationalism is the rebirth of India of the Kshatriya, the samurai.

In 1909, he wrote: "An Indian Nationalism, largely Hindu in its spirit and traditions, because the Hindu made the land and the people and persists, by the greatness of his past, his civilisation and his culture and his invincible virility".

In 1926, Shri Aurobindo wrote: "Did India have the national idea in the modern sense? The 'Nation Idea' India never had. By that I mean the political idea of the nation. It is a modern growth. But we had in India the cultural and spiritual idea of the nation."

Bal Gangadhar Tilak is most remembered for his thundering declaration "*Swaraaj* is my birthright". Although a member of the Indian National Congress, he had, according to Dr Parshotam Mehra, (professor of history at the Punjab University), a profound respect for Hindu tradition, religion, philosophy and ethics. The *Gita Rahasya* is a monument to his scholarship. But he did not merely comment on the Gita; he lived it.

Tilak tried to arouse national pride and Hindu unity by revitalising well known religious festivals, and resurrecting forgotten national heroes.

Thus, in 1893, he revived the Ganapati festival and two years later the Shivaji festival. He later refuted the charge that his propagation of these celebrations had any anti-Muslim inspiration. His prime motive was to unite all Indians.

Veer Savarkar's magnum opus *Hindutva* was the first serious effort to define this concept of cultural nationalism. The book was published first in 1923 when Savarkar was in Ratanagiri jail. Its authorship was therefore, ascribed to "A Maratha". The ideas however, were formed over the many years since 1906 when he was studying law in England.

A Hindu, according to Vinayak Damodar Savarkar, is anyone who acknowledges Hindustan as his fatherland or *pitribhu* as well as his holy land, *punyabhu*. Whether he or she is a devotee of Sanatana Dharma is unimportant; anyone who himself or his ancestor was born in undivided India and who is even a Buddhist, whomsoever's ancestor was a Hindu but was converted to, say, Islam or Christianity is also welcome back to the Hindu fold, provided he accepts India as his fatherland-cum-holy land.

Hindutva is not a word but a history. Hinduism is only a derivative, a fraction or a part of Hindutva or Hinduness. Common blood, common culture, common customs and laws, common history—all add up to Hindutva, according to Savarkar. His exercise in definition was novel and well thought out. It was an intellectual effort and influenced by the European ideas and idioms of his day.

To that extent, Savarkar's thinking was not as deeply rooted in the Indian soil as that of, say, Swami Vivekananda, who felt that Asians proceed from religion to politics and unlike the Euro-Americans the other way around. To us India is mother and not father. Fatherland is a German and Russian idiom.

Mahatma Gandhi understood the Hindu psyche like the back of his palm. He could therefore, move the masses of India more than anyone else before or after him. Although he was no orator, his contribution to development of Hindutva as an ideology was much less than his exemplary insight into how the collective Hindu thinks and feels. If this experience is used appropriately it could bring a more widespread following for the cause of Hindutva.

It is instructive to look at how he was able to appeal to the people of India and win their faith. He quit *sansar*, became a celibate and let it be known widely. That was his last gesture of *tyaag*. Yet he did not don *bhagwa* or saffron clothes. Such sanyasis were cheaper by the dozen and Gandhi might have been misunderstood as a hypocrite. To be seen to be a *tyaagi* is crucial in our country. In the eyes of the people at large it is a testimonial of being a person of integrity. Indians have implicitly trusted legitimate monarchs or leaders who are known to have made a sacrifice.

The Mahatma chose non-violent non-co-operation because Indians, especially the Hindus, abhor violence. Some young men and women might have volunteered to take to the gun but the masses could not have come to agitate on the streets; certainly not women, children or even older men.

He conveyed to the people living even in remote villages what freedom was all about with the help of the *charkha* and *khadi*. Remember, the media available in his days was very limited. Indeed he completely understood the Hindu psyche.

Keshav Baliram Hedgewar was described by Guruji Madhavrao Sadashivrao Golwalkar as a child of greatness. He went on to write that the greatest of men who grace the world stage often cast that spell to make others unaware of their greatness so that they may not shirk and shudder at their greatness but come and freely mix with them in a spirit of comradeship. Sri Krishna by his childish pranks had cast a spell over everyone in Gokul near Mathura. None, not even Yashoda, would remember that he was an *avatar*. Once when he was reported to have eaten dust and Yashoda forced him to open his mouth, she saw illimitable universes dancing in that little cavity. She was shocked and dumbfounded. But that was only for the moment. The same old smiling, mischievous, teasing pranks of the child Krishna made her forget that fleeting realisation. Doctor Hedgewar's disarming simplicity had cast a similar spell upon all those who came near him, even his closest friends and co-workers. It was only rarely that they would remember, as if in a flash, that they were in the company of a great soul of unsurpassable majesty, born but once in centuries for the redemption of the people. And they would be surprised at the free and almost equal way in which they mixed with him, sometimes even taking liberties with him. But that was all for a moment. Again the simple, smiling figure of the Doctor would cast its spell and they would forget all about it. Such was the Doctor, the Hindu ideal of a man in flesh and blood: the embodiment of the saying that the great ones achieve great tasks not because of external aids but by their intrinsic merit, a guiding light for all generations to fashion their lives in its effulgence for glorious and immortal national life.

Guruji Golwalkar: In describing the bedrock of national integration, we often hear our political leaders speaking of national integration, emotional integration and so on. But what is that common emotion, that basis on which all can come together? What are those eternal life springs of our national life that go to make it unified, resurgent and glorious? These are:

> In the first place, the feeling of burning devotion to the land which, from time immemorial, we have regarded as our sacred *matrubhoomi*.
>
> In the second place, the feeling of fellowship of fraternity, born out of the realisation that we are the children of that one great common Mother.
>
> In the third place, the intense awareness of a common culture and heritage, of common history and traditions, of common ideals and aspirations.

This trinity of values or, in a word, Hindu nationalism, forms that bedrock of our national edifice.

On the other hand, the idea of domination through brute strength is absolutely alien to our culture and tradition. Our whole being revolts against this un-Hindu concept. Numerous faiths and creeds have flourished here from ancient times. We have had a variegated pattern of political institutions. We have had republican governments and hereditary kingships. Under all conditions the people were free to follow their healthy persuasions in every walk of life. Everyone was encouraged to develop himself according to his individual genius, nature and inclination. In keeping with that spirit, the work of the Hindu missionaries for rousing and organising the society has always been through love and service, character and sacrifice and never through brute force or political power.

In the words of Prof Sitaram Chaturvedi, the Banaras Hindu University is, quite literally, the creation of Pandit Madan Mohan Malaviya. With the establishment of the universities at Mumbai, Kolkata, Chennai, Lahore and Allahabad, a new class of young men came up in India, whose ambition was to secure administrative jobs under the British government.

In the light of these developments, it became necessary to establish a national university where oriental and occidental arts, humanities and sciences could be taught without losing contact with Indian culture and thought. In the year 1904, Malaviya formally moved the resolution for establishing a Hindu University at a meeting held in Banaras.

Pandit Malaviya was a committed nationalist who, evidently felt that one sure way of capturing the ground for Hindutva was to educate young minds. The contribution of the university is well known.

Sardar Vallabhbhai Patel's contribution to the future of Hindutva can be imagined only if we recall that, on the eve of partition, about two/fifths of the Indian territory was ruled by some 565 princes. These were independent rulers, subject only to the British Crown being paramount or suzerain. While decisions were going to be made, one British proposal was to divide India three ways: Hindustan, Pakistan and Princestan, the last comprising of these states.

Fortunately, this plan got overruled when the well-known June 3 Plan was evolved, on the basis of which the Independence of India Bill was passed by the British

Parliament. Only a few princely states happened to be located within the territory that was eventually demarcated for Pakistan.

Upon the departure of the British on 14 August 1947, the paramountcy was to lapse. This meant that the states became technically free to join either Hindustan or Pakistan or even declare independence as indeed the Nizam of Hyderabad tried to do.

Mohammad Ali Jinnah expected not only Kashmir, Hyderabad and Bhopal to join his new dominion but also Indore, Jodhpur, Junagadh, Jamnagar and even Baroda. Sardar Patel was the Home Minister as well as the Minister of States (princely). The entire responsibility, therefore, fell upon him to invite, to persuade, to cajole, to coerce, to threaten all these states which lay within the boundary of Hindustan.

Hyderabad was the only state against which some force had to be used. For the rest, it was achieved by the tact, dedication and determination of Vallabhbhai Patel. Since he succeeded with aplomb within a few months, his achievements have tended to be taken for granted. Imagine the disaster had he wavered or failed! The map of India could have seemed tragically like a sieve. The Sardar was a nationalist, for which the Nehruites criticised him by insinuating that he was communal.

It is this type of elastic and self-expressive pattern of organisation that has helped our society to keep alive its spirit of coherence in spite of being subjected to unparalleled atrocities and aggressions. If the pattern had been rigid and imposed from above, our society would have today remained merely as a fossil, just as some of the huge animals became immobile and gradually perished under the dead weight of their rigid protective covers. The devotees of Hindutva have therefore, rightly eschewed all such self-defeating alien types of organisations and stuck to our pure and healthy national system for rebuilding society.

The word fundamentalism was first used to describe the conservative Christian who referred to the holy Bible as his argument to resist Darwin's theory of evolution. Since Hinduism has nothing comparable to the Bible, its followers cannot be a fundamentalists.

This word was first used in our country in the wake of Sant Bhindranwale turning militant around 1983.

Indira Gandhi and, in fact, all her supporters had to find a special word to condemn him and his fellowmen. They could not use the word communal because, in their idiom, the expression was earmarked for the devotees of Hindutva. They promptly imported the word fundamentalist from the USA.

The Americans had exhumed it in order to abuse Ayatollah Khomeini who had thrown out Washington's favourite Reza Shah Pahlavi from the throne of Iran. There is a reason why I have used the word exhumed. Fundamentalism had for decades been forgotten in the United States. It had come into prominence after World War I and, after a few years, had fallen into disuse.

The theory of evolution by Charles Darwin had crossed the Atlantic and gained currency in the USA. Many people, including the liberals among the priests, began to appreciate Darwin's contention. His great work, *On the origin of species by means of natural selection, or the preservation of favoured races in the struggle for life* had been published in England in 1859. A storm of protest soon arose over the book, reaching its height at Oxford in 1860 when a scientist called TH Huxley and Bishop Wilberforce fought a gun duel. The acceptance of the new theory threatened to pull the carpet from under the biblical doctrine of creation.

14

What the World Says About Hindudom

It is both essential and instructive to learn what the world's eminences from the fields of scholarship and politics, spread across the span of history and time and belonging to different nations and diverse backgrounds, have had to say about Hinduism and its philosophy.

Will Durant, (American historian and philosopher): "India was the motherland of our race, and Sanskrit the mother of Europe's languages. She was the mother of our philosophy; mother, through the Arabs, of much of our mathematics; mother, through the Buddha, of the ideals embodied in Christianity; mother, through the village community, of self-government and democracy. It is true that even across the Himalayan barrier India has sent to the West such gifts as grammar and logic, philosophy and fables, hypnotism and chess, and above all numerals and the decimal system. India will teach us the tolerance and gentleness of mature mind, understanding spirit and a unifying, pacifying love for all human beings. Mother India is in many ways the mother of us all".

Mark Twain, (American author): "India is the cradle of the human race, the birthplace of human speech, the mother of history, the grandmother of legend, and the great-grandmother of tradition. Our most valuable and most instructive materials in the history of man are treasured up in India only. So far as I am able to judge, nothing has been left undone, either by man or nature, to make India the most extraordinary country that the sun visits on his rounds. Nothing seems to have been forgotten, nothing overlooked. India has two million gods and worships them all. In religion all other countries are paupers; India is the only millionaire".

Max Mueller, (German scholar): "If I were asked under what sky the human mind has most fully developed some of its choicest gifts, has most deeply pondered on the greatest problems of life, and has found solutions, I should point to India. Further, in the *Sacred Books of the East*, Mueller had said, 'There is no book in the world that is so thrilling, stirring and inspiring as the Upanishads."

Romain Rolland, (French scholar): "If there is one place on the face of earth where all the dreams of living men have found a home from the very earliest days when man began the dream of existence, it is India".

Albert Einstein, (Scientist): "We owe a lot to the Indians, who taught us how to count, without which no worthwhile scientific discovery could have been made".

Henry David Thoreau, (American thinker and author): "Whenever I have read any part of the Vedas, I have felt that some unearthly and unknown light illuminated me. In the great teaching of the Vedas, there is no touch of sectarianism. It is of all ages, climbs, and nationalities and is the royal road for the attainment of the great knowledge.

When I read it, I feel that I am under the spangled heavens of a summer night".

Ralph Waldo Emerson, (American author): "In the great books of India, an empire spoke to us, nothing small or unworthy, but large, serene, consistent, the voice of an old intelligence, which in another age and climate had pondered and thus, disposed of the questions that exercise us".

Hu Shih, (former Chinese Ambassador to the USA): "India conquered and dominated China culturally for 20 centuries without ever having to send a single soldier across her border".

Keith Bellows, (National Geographic Society): "There are some parts of the world that, once visited, get into your heart and won't go. For me, India is such a place. When I first visited, I was stunned by the richness of the land, by its lush beauty and exotic architecture, by its ability to overload the senses with the pure, concentrated intensity of its colours, smells, tastes, and sounds. I had been seeing the world in black and white and, when brought face-to-face with India, experienced everything re-rendered in brilliant technicolour (*A Rough Guide to India*).It is impossible not to be astonished by India. Nowhere on earth does humanity present itself in such a dizzying, creative burst of cultures and religions, races and tongues. Enriched by successive waves of migration and marauders from distant lands, every one of them left an indelible imprint, which was absorbed into the Indian way of life. Every aspect of the country presents itself on a massive, exaggerated scale, worthy in comparison only to the superlative mountains that overshadow it. It is this variety which provides a breathtaking ensemble for experiences that is uniquely Indian. Perhaps the only thing more difficult than to be indifferent to India would be to describe or understand India completely. There are perhaps very few nations in the world with the enormous variety that India has to offer. Modern day India represents the largest democracy in the world with a seamless picture of unity in diversity unparalleled anywhere else".

William James, (American author): "From the Vedas, we learn a practical art of surgery, medicine, music, house building under which mechanized art is included. They are encyclopaedia of every aspect of life, culture, religion, science, ethics, law, cosmology and meteorology".

Dr Arnold Toynbee, (British historian): "It is already becoming clear that a chapter which had a Western beginning will have to have an Indian ending if it is not to end in the self-destruction of the human race. At this supremely dangerous moment in history, the only way of salvation for mankind is the Indian way".

Sir William Jones, (British Orientalist): "The Sanskrit language, whatever be its antiquity, is of wonderful structure, more perfect than the Greek, more copious than the Latin and more exquisitely refined than either".

Peter Johnstone, (British mathematician): "Gravitation was known to the Hindus (Indians) before the birth of Newton. The system of blood circulation was discovered by them centuries before Harvey was heard of".

Emmeline Plunket, (Author, in *Calendars and Constellations*): "They were very advanced Hindu astronomers in 6000 BC. The Vedas contain an account of the dimension of earth, the sun, moon, planets and galaxies".

Sylvain Levi, (French Orientologist and Indologist): "She (India) has left indelible imprints on one-fourth of the human race in the course of a long succession of centuries. She has the right to reclaim her place amongst the great nations summarizing and symbolizing the spirit of humanity. From Persia to the Chinese sea, from the icy regions of Siberia to Islands of Java and Borneo, India has propagated her beliefs, her tales, and her civilization!"

Arthur Schopenhauer, German philosopher, in *Works VI*: "The Vedas are the most rewarding and the most elevating book which can be possible in the world".

Colonel James Todd, (British Oriental scholar): "Where can we look for sages like those whose systems of philosophy were prototypes of those of Greece: to whose works Plato, Thales, and Pythagoras were disciples? Where do I find astronomers whose knowledge of planetary systems excites wonder in Europe as well as the architects and sculptors whose works claim our admiration, and the musicians who could make the mind oscillate from joy to sorrow, from tears to smiles with the change of modes and varied intonation?"

Lancelot Hogben, (British zoologist and medical statistician: in *Mathematics for the Millions*): "There has been no more revolutionary contribution than the one which the Hindus made when they invented Zero".

Ella Wheeler Wilcox, (American author and poet): "India—the land of the Vedas, the remarkable works that contain not only religious ideas for a perfect life but also facts which science has proved true. Electricity, radium, electronics, airship, all were known to the seers who founded the Vedas".

Werner Heisenberg, (German physicist): "After the conversations about Indian philosophy, some of the ideas of Quantum Physics that had seemed so crazy suddenly made much more sense".

Dr William Hunter, (British surgeon): "The surgery of the ancient Indian physicians was bold and skilful. A special branch of surgery was dedicated to rhinoplasty or operations for improving deformed ears, noses and forming new ones, which European surgeons have now borrowed".

Sir John Woodroffe, (British Orientalist): "An examination of Indian Vedic doctrines shows that it is in tune with the most advanced scientific and philosophical thought of the West".

VG Rele, (Historian in *The Vedic Gods)*: "Our present knowledge of the nervous system fits in so accurately with the internal description of the human body given in the Vedas (5,000 years ago). Then the question arises whether the Vedas are really religious books or books on anatomy of the nervous system and medicine".

Adolf Seilachar, (German palaeontologist and) **PK Bose,** (Indian physicist): "One billion year old fossils prove life began in India". (Associated Free Press, Washington, reports in *Science Magazine* that German palaeontologist Adolf Seilachar and Indian scientist PK Bose have unearthed fossil in Churhat, a town in Madhya Pradesh, India, which is 1.1 billion years old and has rolled back the evolutionary clock by more than 500 million years.

Index

D

E

F

G

H

N

O

P

Q

R

T

Y

Z